Great Psalms of the Bible

Also available from Westminster John Knox Press

Great Prayers of the Old Testament by Walter Brueggemann

Also by J. Clinton McCann Jr. from Westminster John Knox Press

Judges (Interpretation series)

Great Psalms
of the Bible

J. Clinton McCann Jr.

WESTMINSTER
JOHN KNOX PRESS
LOUISVILLE · KENTUCKY

Unless otherwise indicated, Scripture quotations are from the New Revised Standard Version of the Bible, copyright © 1989 by the Division of Christian Education of the National Council of the Churches of Christ in the U.S.A., and are used by permission.

Book design by Sharon Adams
Cover design by Jennifer Cox
Cover photo: © *Jutta Klee/Corbis*

First edition
Published by Westminster John Knox Press
Louisville, Kentucky

This book is printed on acid-free paper that meets the American National Standards Institute Z39.48 standard. ∞

PRINTED IN THE UNITED STATES OF AMERICA

09 10 11 12 13 14 15 16 17 18 — 10 9 8 7 6 5 4 3 2 1

Library of Congress Cataloging-in-Publication Data

McCann, J. Clinton
    Great Psalms of the Bible / J. Clinton McCann, Jr. — 1st ed.
        p. cm. — (Great texts series)
    Includes bibliographical references.
    ISBN 978-0-664-23176-7 (alk. paper)
    1. Bible. O.T. Psalms—Criticism, interpretation, etc. I. Title.

BS1430.52.M43 2009
223'.206—dc22

2008039363

For my wife, Sarah, one of the pastors
of Hope United Church of Christ in St. Louis,
and for my children—Jennifer, Sarah, Annalise, and Ian—
with profound gratitude and deep affection

Contents

Acknowledgments

Although I cannot mention them by name, I am grateful to the hundreds of groups and thousands of individuals with whom I have had the pleasure of teaching and learning about the Psalms over the past twenty-one years. These include classes at Eden Theological Seminary, adult education classes in scores of congregations, participants in dozens of retreats and workshops sponsored by various church judicatories and church-related bodies, my scholarly colleagues who participate in the Book of Psalms program unit of the Society of Biblical Literature, and more. Special thanks are due to two groups who helped me directly in my preparation of this volume: my friends (all Old Testament scholars like myself) in a study group called *Lemadim Olam* (Students Forever), who offered helpful and constructive criticism of chapters 1 and 2 of this work; and the Adult Bible Study group at the New Piasa Chautauqua (along the Mississippi River, between Grafton and Elsah, Illinois), which participated with me during the summer season of 2007 in a study of the twelve psalms covered in this work. Chautauquans Mary and Bob Street graciously made available their front porch for our sessions, and Chautauquan Larry Colbert took a special interest in this project, performing the valuable service of keeping me and the group focused on the question of the relevance of the Psalms for today (see the "For Today" sections below in the treatment of each psalm).

Thanks too to my faculty colleagues and the Board of Directors of Eden Theological Seminary for granting me a sabbatical leave during the fall semester of 2007, during which I did much of the writing of this book; to Caron Strother, administrative assistant to the Eden faculty, for her constant attentiveness to all my requests for help; and to Jon Berquist at Westminster John Knox Press for extending to me the invitation to undertake this project, for advising me along the way, and for guiding it to completion.

Finally, thanks to my wife, Sarah, and my children—Jennifer, Sarah, Annalise, and Ian—for their love, encouragement, patience, and support. It is to them that I dedicate this book.

Clint McCann

Chapter One

Psalm 1

L ike the first line, paragraph, or chapter of any book, Psalm 1 is extraordinarily important. Along with Psalm 2, to which it is linked literarily by the repetition of "happy" in the opening line of Psalm 1 and the closing line of Psalm 2, Psalm 1 introduces the book of Psalms. It is significant that the very first word in the book of Psalms is "happy," a word that will recur twenty-five more times in the Psalms. In a real sense, the entire book is a portrayal of the shape and character of genuine happiness, and as we shall see, the way that the Psalms describe happiness is in sharp contrast to the views of happiness in contemporary North American culture. Indeed, this disconnect is one of the primary things that make the Psalms so critically important for today. Perhaps the Psalms can help to reorient us, so that our persistent pursuit of happiness will be more satisfying and fulfilling, rather than leaving us tired, empty, and discouraged, as it often does for many people.

Besides the word "happy," the other word that virtually jumps off the page at us in the opening verses of Psalm 1 is the word traditionally translated "law." As is often the case in the Psalms and in Hebrew poetry in general, the importance of this word is signaled by its repetition; it occurs twice in verse 2. The underlying Hebrew word is one that many people will have heard before—

torah. While the term *torah* can mean "law" or "legislation," its fundamental sense is something like "instruction" or "teaching," and this is how it should be translated in Psalm 1:2. In fact, the traditional translation "law" has been largely responsible for the fact that many interpreters of Psalm 1 over the years have viewed it in a decidedly negative light. The person who pursues happiness by delighting in the "law," even to the point of meditating upon the "law" round the clock ("day and night"), has been viewed by many commentators as boring and pedantic, and even worse, as self-righteous and legalistic—not a very good way to introduce the book of Psalms!

But if *torah* is heard in its basic sense of "teaching" or "instruction," we get a very different picture of how the psalmist pursues happiness. It does not involve self-righteous legalism but rather the positioning of the self to attend constantly and joyfully to God and God's will. In fact, such a posture is precisely the opposite of legalism and self-righteousness, for it means the living of a thoroughly God-centered, not self-centered, life. And since *torah* can mean something as broad as "unmediated divine teaching,"[1] the psalmist's pursuit of happiness will involve unwavering attention to God and ongoing discernment of what God might say to him or lead him to do next. Again, such openness to God is diametrically opposed to legalism. And as for allegedly being boring or pedantic, what could be more exciting and challenging than living not simply for oneself but for God and in accordance with God's purposes for humankind and for the world?

All of the above—the emphasis in the opening lines of Psalm 1 on happiness and instruction—suggests that Psalm 1 and the way it introduces the book of Psalms should be heard in an overwhelmingly positive light. Psalm 1 is known among scholars as a *torah psalm* (see also Psalms 19, 119), and this is a helpful designation. That is, Psalm 1 intends to teach, and as an introduction to the book of Psalms, it orients the reader to expect to learn from all the Psalms. In particular, what we as readers are invited and encouraged to look and listen for—and what this volume and its treatment of the Psalms will attempt to highlight—is instruction on how to live the way God wants humans to live. In other words, we shall attempt to focus on how our living may serve to glorify God. This focus will involve regular attention to a set of related questions: Who is God? Who are we as human beings? How does God relate to the world, including us human beings? And how does God want us to respond? In short, what is the shape of the faithful life, the life lived under God's claim, and hence, in accordance with God's will? Our consideration of these questions will regularly take place with an eye toward the realities, issues, and challenges of our contemporary world.

Unlike most of the psalms, Psalm 1 is neither praise nor prayer. In all likelihood, most of the psalms—the songs of praise and the prayers for help—originated to be used in worship. In fact, the Psalms have been used in Jewish and Christian worship for centuries and still are being used as songs of praise and prayers in liturgical settings. To be sure, liturgy itself is instructional. We learn from the songs we sing and from the prayers that we pray or that we hear others pray. Worship orients us, and it directs our lives and loyalties. As a *torah* psalm that introduces a collection consisting primarily of songs of praise and prayers, Psalm 1 reinforces and extends the instructional intent of the book of Psalms. As one scholar puts it, the book of Psalms may have served originally in ancient Israel and Judah as a hymn book or prayer book, but it was ultimately transmitted and received among the people of God as something like a catechism or "instruction manual," to be read and meditated upon beyond formal liturgical settings.[2]

To put it somewhat differently, the book of Psalms may have originated primarily as a record of and means of facilitating the human response to God; however, it has also been transmitted and received among the people of God as God's word to humankind. In short, the book of Psalms is Scripture, and as with all books of the Bible, we should expect the book of Psalms to teach us about God, about human identity in relationship to God, and about the shape and character of the faithful life. The effect of Psalm 1 is precisely to reinforce this expectation, as well as to create a sense of anticipation. The remainder of the book of Psalms will not disappoint. As James L. Mays points out, the Psalms "contain more direct statements about God than any other book in the two testaments of the Christian canon."³ In fact, Psalm 1:6 is the Psalter's first direct statement about God. So, Psalm 1 not only invites and orients the reader to be ready to learn, but it also begins the actual instruction, further aspects of which we shall consider in the next section.

Dimensions of Meaning

Verse 1

It is somewhat surprising that Psalm 1 begins by defining happiness negatively, but there appears to be a reason for this. In any case, the rhetorical effect is to set up a sharp contrast between the happy, who will later be called "the righteous" (vv. 5–6), and "the wicked," who also receive further attention in verses 4–6. Not only does the repetition of "the wicked" (four times) serve to emphasize their presence, but so also do the two synonyms in verse 1—"sinners" (see also v. 5) and "scoffers." Again, the amount of attention devoted to "the wicked" may be surprising, but in this regard, Psalm 1 is performing part of its introductory function—that is, the prevalence of "the wicked" in Psalm 1 signals the fact that "the wicked" will be a pervasive presence throughout the book of Psalms, especially in the prayers, which are concentrated in Books I–II (Pss. 1–72; see the chapter on Ps. 73). The vocabulary will vary—"the wicked" are also called "enemies," "foes," "adversaries," "evildoers," and so on—but they are always there.

Who are "the wicked"? In short, they are those who constantly oppose God and God's will, and because "the righteous" are those who are attentive to God and God's will, "the wicked" constantly oppose "the righteous" as well. The term "scoffers" in verse 1 is a helpful clue to the character of "the wicked." It occurs most often in the book of Proverbs, which is didactic literature, and refers to those who refuse to be taught. Thus, "the wicked" will clearly not attend to God's "instruction" (nor to anyone else's perhaps). Rather, they are those who choose to go it alone. The several quotations of "the wicked" in the book of Psalms also reveal their character. In fact, "the wicked" speak as early as the second verse of the first prayer in the Psalter, and they say to the faithful, "There is no help for you in God" (Ps. 3:2). Elsewhere, they similarly deny God's existence and governance (see Pss. 10:4, 13; 14:1; 73:11), preferring instead to rely on themselves and their own resources, while pursuing their own agendas rather than God's will (see Ps. 10:6). In a word, wickedness is extreme *autonomy*—self-assertion and self-directedness—over against God and God's teaching.

This definition of "the wicked" helps to avoid a possible misunderstanding of the character of the happy or "the righteous." "The righteous" are not those who get everything or do everything right. In short, they are not sinless, as verses 1 and 5 in particular may seem to suggest. Rather, the happy or "the righteous" are those who, because they attend constantly to God and God's teaching, live in fundamental dependence upon God rather than upon themselves and their own resources. Other psalms will clearly demonstrate that "the righteous" can and do sin (see the chapters on Ps. 32 and 51; see also Ps. 143:2). What distinguishes "the righteous" from "the wicked" is that "the righteous" confront and confess their sin, relying ultimately upon God for forgiveness and life. As Jerome Creach sums it up, "The righteous in the Psalms are those who have a right relationship with God and whose relationships with other people are governed by God's expectations for human community.⁴ According to Psalm 1 and the entire book of Psalms, this right relationship with God makes all the difference. In this regard, it is not coincidental that "happy," the first word in Psalm 1, begins with the first letter of the Hebrew alphabet, whereas "perish," the final word in Psalm 1, begins with the final letter of the Hebrew alphabet. The rhetorical effect again is to emphasize in the most comprehensive way possible the contrast between "the righteous"and "the wicked." Attending constantly to God and God's teaching, and living in dependence upon God, are the ways to life. Ignoring God and God's teaching, and living in dependence upon the self and one's own resources, are the ways to death. The contrast could hardly be drawn more sharply.

Verse 2

We have already suggested the crucial importance of the word *torah*, which is presented as a source of joy (see also Ps. 119:1)— indeed, of life itself (see also Ps. 19:7, where the NRSV's "soul" is better understood as "life"). Not surprisingly, the word *torah* is important beyond the Psalms as well. The books of Genesis through Deuteronomy are known among Jews as *the* Torah, the first and most authoritative portion of the Jewish canon. The Torah does contain "law" in the narrow sense of rules and regulations, but it also contains stories that put the various law codes in the context of God's ongoing claim upon and relationship not only with a particular people, Israel, but also with humankind and the whole creation (see Gen. 1–11). Even when the focus is upon law in the narrow sense, the tensions and even contradictions among the various bodies of legislation lead to the conclusion that torah is a "dynamic imperative."[5] That is, attentiveness to torah can never be simply a matter of following rules; rather, it will inevitably be a matter of constant contemplation upon God's comprehensive claim on the whole creation, along with discernment and finally enactment of the implications of God's claim on the whole creation.

So centrally important is torah in the Psalms and elsewhere that Creach even concludes that "torah has become a surrogate for the Lord himself."[6] In short, rejoicing in and meditating upon God's instruction means to be related intimately and inextricably to God's own self. Given the literary links between Psalm 1 and Psalm 2 (in addition to "happy" in 1:1 and 2:12, "meditate" in 1:2 and "plot" in 2:1 translate the same Hebrew word; also see "perish" and "way" in 1:6 and 2:12), which features the king, it is understandable that Deuteronomy 17:18–19 stipulates that the king is always to "have a copy of this law [*torah*]," so that he can read it daily and "*learn* to fear [that is, trust and obey] the LORD his God" (Deut. 17:19; emphasis added). Again, *torah* bespeaks relatedness to God, in terms of submission of the self to God and God's will. Constant meditation on the torah is also enjoined upon Joshua as he succeeds Moses (see Josh 1:8, which, like Ps. 1:2, includes the phrase "day and night"). Although the torah is specifically a "book" in Joshua 1:8, the intent of torah meditation is to ensure the ongoing relatedness of Joshua and the people to God after Moses' death. The word used in Joshua 1:9 to describe the results of such relatedness is "prosperous," representing a Hebrew root that also underlies "prosper" in Psalm 1:3, part of the central section of the psalm to which we now turn.

Verses 3–4

The central section of Psalm 1 consists of two contrasting similes. Although "the wicked" are given emphasis by the repetition of "wicked" in verses 1, 4, 5, and 6, the central section of Psalm 1 gives more attention to those who attend to God's teaching. They receive three full poetic lines, whereas "the wicked" are allotted only one and one-half lines. Further attention is drawn to this central section by the fact that the key words in the similes— "trees" and "chaff"—are both two-letter Hebrew nouns that share a common final consonant.

Trees that are planted or transplanted by streams of water obviously have a better chance of surviving and being fruitful, as the simile suggests. Such a location, however, does not guarantee that all circumstances will be ideal. Thus, the final line of the first simile, "In all that they do, they prosper," can be misleading, especially the word "prosper." For North Americans, the words "prosper" and "prosperity" inevitably seem to suggest money or material wealth, but this is not the point at all. A better translation would be something like "thrives" (JPS). In any case, to prosper here connotes connectedness to God, not wealth or material well-being in every circumstance. In fact, as suggested above, "the righteous" in the book of Psalms are regularly opposed by "the wicked," so much so that "the righteous" are typically named in the Psalms by words such as "afflicted," "oppressed," "needy," "poor," "helpless," and so on. In the midst of affliction, however, the happiness of "the righteous" consists in taking "refuge" in God (see, e.g., Pss. 2:12; 7:1; 11:1; 16:1). They continue to survive and thrive because of their connectedness to God.

The simile in verse 3 is very similar to the one in Jeremiah

17:7–8, which specifically mentions something not found in Psalm 1—that is, the rootedness of "a tree planted by water." Rootedness, of course, suggests connectedness, the real point of the simile in verse 3. It is revealing to note as well that the simile in Jeremiah 17:7–8 involves those "who trust in the LORD." The near identity of the two similes reinforces the conclusion that for the psalmist, constant attention to God's torah is, indeed, related-ness to God's own self. Again, connectedness is of the essence.

The simile in verse 3 also bears some resemblance to the ones in Psalms 52:8 and 92:12–15, which both involve trees. In these latter two cases, however, the righteous are like trees planted "in the house of God" (Ps. 52:8; 92:13 is nearly identical)—that is, the temple. Jerome Creach suggests that Psalm 1:3 at least hints at a temple setting, by way of the particular Hebrew word underlying "streams," a word elsewhere associated clearly with the mythical river flowing from the Temple Mount. But the failure to mention explicitly the temple in Psalm 1 is very revealing, since this very omission suggests that delight in and constant meditation upon God's torah enables one to experience God's presence just as tan-gibly as a visit to the temple, God's own house. As suggested above, in Creach's words again, "torah has become a surrogate for the Lord himself." Connectedness is crucial. To attend constantly to God's teaching is to experience God's real presence, to be truly in relationship with God.

This experience of and relationship with God is precisely what the wicked miss, as suggested by the emphatic adversative that begins verse 4 (the Hebrew more literally is "Not so the wicked"). Contrary to how the simile in verse 4 is often understood, it is not a matter of God actively "blowing away" the wicked. Rather, the wicked themselves have chosen not to attend to God and God's teaching. Thus, they have missed the chance to be rooted in God and nurtured toward fruitfulness. Like chaff which is light—recall again the lighter attention given to the wicked in verses 3–4—and thus subject to being blown by the wind, the wicked have no foun-dation, no stable location, no rootedness for the long run. The point of the two similes in verses 3–4 involves as much the issue of *location* as it does the matter of fruitfulness. In this regard, verses

3–4 recall verse 1, where the three verbs used to indicate the activity of the "happy" are location words—"walk" (NRSV, "follow"), "stand" (NRSV, "take"), and "sit." In short, location is crucial! Where one chooses to locate oneself makes all the difference. For Psalm 1, the book of Psalms, and the Bible in general, locating oneself in relationship to God means enduring happiness and life; choosing alienation from God means destruction and death.

Verses 5–6

The traditional translation of verse 5, reflected in the NRSV, has proven problematic for commentators, especially given the introductory function of Psalm 1. Which "judgment" does the psalmist have in mind? Given the usual dating of the compilation of the book of Psalms, the so-called Last Judgment seems anachronistic and thus very unlikely. Furthermore, given the pervasive presence of the enemies in the Psalms, it does not appear that God acts retributively to eliminate them, as verse 5 seems to suggest in the traditional rendering. To be sure, verse 5 may articulate the hope for and trust in the ultimate fulfillment of God's purposes for the world—that is, the wicked will not finally prevail as they seem to do for now (see Ps. 73). In this case, no particular judgment is in view; rather, the psalmist here, as the psalmists regularly do, entrusts life and future to God. This may be the proper understanding of verse 5, but there may also be another possibility.

The Hebrew of verse 5a reads literally, "The wicked will not stand (up) in(to) judgment/justice." The syntax is difficult, but given the context of *torah* (v. 2), and given that God's will is summarized elsewhere in the Psalms as "justice" (see Pss. 72:1–7; 82:1–4; as well as 96:9 and 98:9, where "judge" is better translated "establish justice"), it seems at least possible that the sense of verse 5a is this: "The wicked will not stand up for justice." In this case, verse 5 is not a comment about God's retributive action toward the wicked but rather a comment about the wicked's choice to ignore God and God's teaching. The wicked will not stand up for justice, because they refuse to attend to God and to what God wills for the world. They will not stand "in the congregation of the righteous," not because God keeps them out but because they refuse to enter. If this is a possible interpretive direction, then again, where one chooses to locate oneself is crucial, as in verses 1–4.

Similarly, verse 6 may be understood relationally rather than retributively. The word that the NRSV translates as "watches" is more literally "knows," and it is a word used regularly in the Old Testament to express relationship. By virtue of their attentiveness to God's teaching, "the righteous" enjoy the connectedness to God that means true happiness and life. In contrast, "the wicked . . . perish," not because God has rejected them but because they have chosen to reject God. This relational construal is captured effectively by the CEV: "the wicked follow a road that leads to ruin." As suggested earlier, the first and last words of Psalm 1— "happy" and "perish"—reinforce sharply the contrasting alternatives that have been presented throughout the psalm. Psalm 1 thus invites us readers to choose as well—in particular, to choose to pursue happiness not by doing what we want but by doing what God wills. In a context like ours, this invitation amounts to a colossal challenge.

Psalm 1 for Today

The 1970s were known as the "Me Decade," and writer Walker Percy labeled the entire twentieth century as "the Century of the Self."[7] It seems that the twenty-first century is no different. For instance, *Time* magazine named "You" as its 2006 "Person of the Year" and included on the cover of the December 25, 2006–January 1, 2007 edition a little mirror in which each reader could view herself or himself. In commenting upon their choice, the editors say on the cover, "Yes, you. You control the Information Age. Welcome to your world." To be sure, they go on to suggest that the focus on "You" has great positive potential. The power of "You," in conjunction with the power of the World Wide Web, is "a story about community and collaboration on a scale never seen before. . . . This is an opportunity to build a new kind of international understanding, not politician to politician, great man to great man, but citizen to citizen, person to person."[8]

Perhaps this assessment is correct, but a *Time* essay from 2004 is much less optimistic and much more sobering. Entitled "The Age of iPod Politics: The Niching of America Makes for Happy Consumers and Angry Voters," its basic point is that our ability to focus entirely on ourselves and create our own little worlds makes the art of politics—that is, the creation of community—very difficult. As the author, James Poniewozik, puts it, "We are the America of the iPod ads—stark, black silhouettes tethered by our brilliant white earbuds, rocking out passionately and alone. You make your choices, and I make mine. Yours, of course, are wrong. But what do I care?"[9] In short, the danger of highlighting "You" as "Person of the Year" is that we simply legitimate and encourage selfishness and isolation.

The Onion, a publication that offers a humorous and satirical view of the news, captures this danger well in the following "report" in its March 9, 2005, edition:

> The "Me Decade," a period beginning in the 1970s and marked by self-awareness and self-fulfillment, celebrated its 35th year Monday. "With careerism, materialism, and general self-involvement as popular as they were decades ago, the Me Decade may well go on for another 35 years," said historian and Columbia University professor Dr. Vera Concklin. "It's been the longest-running decade in American history, beating the selfless 'Greatest Generation' of the '40s by a good 15 years. Selfishness, it seems, is here to stay." Author Tom Wolfe, who coined the term in his essay "The Me Decade and the Third Great Awakening," was unavailable for comment, as he is working on his memoirs.[10]
>

To be sure, selfishness and self-assertion have always been a problem in human history (see Gen. 3), but coupled with our incredible affluence, our range of options, and our dazzling technology in contemporary North America, the danger is that we will raise selfishness to a whole new level.

On a more serious note, this is exactly what we are doing, according to clinical psychologist and best-selling author Mary Pipher. She identifies our current me-oriented direction and its consequences as a crisis, which she describes using the word "happy," the word that begins Psalm 1:

> We have a crisis in meaning in our culture. The crisis comes from our isolation from each other, from the values we learn in a culture of consumption and from the fuzzy, self-help message that the only commitment is to the self and the only important question is—Am I happy? We learn that we are number one and that our own immediate needs are the most important ones. The crisis comes from the message that products satisfy and that happiness can be purchased.[11]

If happiness in our culture is in danger of being reduced to buying what we want, then it is understandable that philosopher James Edwards suggests that the most appropriate symbol for contemporary North American life is "the regional shopping mall."[12] Of course, there are worse places than malls, as Edwards readily admits, but the danger of defining ourselves by an endless array of products for purchase consists of addiction, boredom, and conformity (what he calls "the triumph of the normal"), none of which bode well either for genuine and enduring individual happiness or for the formation of healthy and constructive community life.[13] Thus, Edwards's assessment confirms Pipher's diagnosis of our contemporary crisis.

In the midst of this crisis of meaning, Psalm 1 cries out to be heard and heeded. To us contemporary folk, for whom the overriding temptation is to define happiness in terms of what we want and what we can purchase, Psalm 1 offers a clear and compelling alternative. Happiness, it affirms, begins not with ourselves and what we want, but rather with God and what God wants. Whereas our misguided pursuit of happiness is producing isolation, alienation, addiction, boredom, and conformity, Psalm 1 invites a pursuit of happiness that promises relationship with God and with one another. Torah, God's teaching, is all about justice and righteousness, which are inherently relational concepts and which ultimately invite us to participate in a community that is nothing short of universe-encompassing (see Pss. 8 and 148). As the Psalms recognize, the cost of participating in God's expansive community is suffering (see the chapters on Pss. 8 and 13), from which there will be no need to try to anesthetize ourselves; there will be no danger of addiction. The challenges of this cosmic community may be overwhelming, but boredom and conformity will be out of the question as we engage in the exhilarating call of attending to the ongoing revelation of God's torah, God's "dynamic imperative"— that is, as we discern what God may say to us next and where God may be leading us and our world today and tomorrow.

It is probably not coincidental that the final psalm of Book I (Pss. 1–41) also begins with the word "happy": "Happy are those who consider the poor." Since the book of Psalms will eventually define the essence of divinity as advocacy for the poor, weak, and needy (see Ps. 82, especially vv. 1–4), Psalm 41:1 essentially says again what Psalm 1 has affirmed—namely, genuine happiness consists in doing God's will, not our own.

This message is reinforced by Jesus and his teaching. When Jesus was asked about torah, he summarized it in two commandments—love God, and love one's neighbor as oneself (Matt. 22:34–40; Jesus is citing here Deut. 6:5 and Lev. 19:18). As is often pointed out, self is not absent from this equation, but self is clearly in the third position behind God and neighbor. Like Psalm 1, Jesus invites us to a thoroughly God-centered life, one that will inevitably be lived for others and not just ourselves. It is interesting too, of course, that Jesus' first extended teaching session or sermon, at least according to the Gospel of Matthew (that is, the Sermon on the Mount in Matt. 5–7), begins with the same word as Psalm 1 does—"happy" or "blessed"—and repeats that word in the subsequent Beatitudes. Just as Psalm 1 invites us to pursue happiness in ways that are strikingly countercultural, so do the Beatitudes, as they pronounce "happy" are the "poor in spirit," "those who mourn," "the meek," and so on, concluding with "those who are persecuted for righteousness' sake." For our purposes in studying the Psalms, it is to be noted that the categories of people pronounced "happy" in the Beatitudes correspond precisely with descriptions of "the righteous" in the Psalms (see Ps. 13). Clearly, for Jesus as well as for Psalm 1, happiness has nothing to do with material prosperity or ease of physical circumstances; rather, it is all about connectedness to God and the pursuit of God's will—that is, "righteousness' sake" (Matt. 5:11).

One further note is necessary to make explicit what has been implied already, as we have considered Psalm 1 and its invitation to a thoroughly God-centered life. If wickedness in the Psalms is essentially selfishness, or as suggested above, extreme autonomy, then we need to be clearly aware that our culture systematically values and teaches what the Psalms call wickedness. As Mary Pipher points out, one of the symptoms of our cultural crisis is the fact that words like "autonomy" and "independence" are seen as unambiguously positive.[14] What suffers as a result are things like community, interdependence, caring, and sharing. The root sense of the word "autonomy" should certainly give us pause when we realize that autonomy is often seen today as the culminating mark of maturity in our culture. The word is composed of two Greek words—*auto*, which means "self," and *nomos*, which means "law." (The Greek Old Testament used the word *nomos* to translate the Hebrew word *torah*). In a fundamental sense, then, to be autonomous is to be a "law unto oneself." The fact that we value autonomy so highly, and that we practice it so well, is precisely the reason that we are a culture in crisis, according to Pipher.

From a theological perspective, autonomous folk will have a hard time practicing what my tradition, the Reformed tradition, affirms is the fundamental purpose of human life. I have in mind the first question and answer of the Shorter Catechism (here modified for inclusivity):

> **Question:** What is the chief end of humanity?
>
> **Answer:** Humanity's chief end is to glorify God and enjoy God forever.

Autonomous folk have a difficult time of glorifying anyone or anything beyond their own selves; to them, the notion of enjoying God is virtually, if not completely, nonsensical. Psalm 1 is an invitation to recover the meaning of the concept, and it points the way. We will realize our essential humanity—there will be no crisis of meaning among us!—and we will enjoy God when we delight in God's teaching and pursue what God wants for the world rather than simply what we want. Such thorough God-centeredness—what Jesus calls losing one's life for the sake of the gospel (Mark 8:35)—promises an authentic happiness that suffering cannot diminish, a genuine prosperity that misfortune cannot destroy, and an abundant life that abides securely in the promise that God "knows the way of the righteous" (Ps. 1:6 RSV).

Questions for Reflection and Discussion

1. The Declaration of Independence, one of the founding documents of the United States, suggests that the pursuit of happiness is an "inalienable right." Such an affirmation seems warranted and helpful, but, of course, the document does not suggest how happiness should be pursued. How do you tend to define and pursue happiness? Does an encounter with Psalm 1 affect your thinking? If so, how and why?

2. Mary Pipher concludes that the cultural crisis among us involves the mistaken notion that happiness can be purchased, and she suggests that advertising plays a key role in reinforcing this notion. This seems to be the case, but there are other forces at work to create demand. Consider the following quote from a recent editorial in the *St. Louis Post-Dispatch:* "Pressure to spend . . . comes from an incessant drumbeat of mass media touting the good life through consumption, as well as from the role models of friends, family and co-workers. The message is clear: It's OK to spend more money. In fact, after the terrorist attacks of Sept. 11, 2001, the very act of shopping acquired a patriotic dimension."[15] Assuming that we might be led by Psalm 1 and other biblical material to shop and consume *less*, how do we resist the tremendous

influence of advertising, the mass media, pressure from family and peers, and even appeals to our patriotism?

3. Is there a positive upside to being autonomous? How might we affirm such a dimension of autonomy while avoiding being simply "laws unto ourselves"?

4. Assuming that Jon Levenson is correct that *torah* can mean something as broad as "unmediated divine teaching," Christians might paraphrase such a conclusion in terms of openness to the Holy Spirit. How might we position ourselves to be constantly open to God and God's teaching, including openness to the Holy Spirit?

5. As we have seen, Psalm 1:5a can be translated, "Therefore the wicked will not stand up for justice." But even if this translation is incorrect, there is ample evidence in Psalm 1 that faithfulness has to do with where we locate ourselves, or where we stand in relation to God and others. How might we stand up for justice in our time and place?

Chapter Two

Psalm 8

Psalm 8 has the distinction of being the only biblical text available on the moon. It resides there on a small disk, deposited by the Apollo 11 astronauts in 1969. The leaders of each country in the world had been invited by NASA to make a contribution to the disk, and Pope Paul VI chose Psalm 8.[1] Given that the psalmist's reflections were evoked by a view of the evening sky, including the moon (v. 3), we can agree that Psalm 8 was an exceedingly appropriate choice—not to mention, of course, the fact that the human ability to reach the moon is ample evidence of the "dominion" (v. 6) that God has chosen to share with us.

Psalm 8 is distinctive in other ways as well. Although it is unanimously categorized by biblical scholars as a hymn or song of praise, it is the only song of praise that is also a prayer—that is, God is addressed directly throughout the psalm (see also Ps. 104, another psalm that focuses on creation and in which God is addressed directly for most of the first thirty verses). This distinction explains why Psalm 8 does not display the typical structural pattern of the songs of praise—an invitation to other people (or things) to praise God, who is referred to in the third person, accompanied by an articulation of reasons why God should be praised (see Ps. 117 for a brief example, and see the chapters on Pss. 103 and 148). While the structure of Psalm 8 is not typical

among the songs of praise, it is important, and it suggests a crucial interpretive question that we shall pursue below—namely,
how do we properly understand and assess the importance of the
majestic sovereignty of God (vv. 1, 9) *and* the glorious sovereignty
("dominion") that God has given to humankind (vv. 4–8)?

One final distinction of Psalm 8 is that it is the first song of
praise in the book of Psalms, which in Hebrew is known simply as
"Praises." This alone might serve to establish the significance of
Psalm 8, but there is even more to be said concerning the importance of the placement of Psalm 8 within the Psalter. It seems, for
instance, to offer the thanks and praise the psalmist has promised
in the concluding verse of Psalm 7 (note also the repetition of
"name" in 7:17 and 8:1, further suggesting a link between the two
psalms). In any case, it is striking and important that Psalm 8
affirms not only the majesty of God but also the exalted status of
humankind. It is striking and important precisely because it may
seem quite unexpected after reading the sequence of Psalms 3–7,
all prayers for help, in which the condition of the human psalmist
is characterized by violent opposition (Pss. 3, 5, and 7), "distress"
and "shame" (Ps. 4:1–2), and "languishing," "terror," "moaning,"
and "grief" (Ps. 6:2–3, 6–7). This larger structural pattern, the juxtaposition of Psalms 3–7 and Psalm 8, also suggests a crucial interpretive question that we shall pursue later: What is the coherence
between a weak, needy, suffering humankind and a humanity
"crowned . . . with glory and honor" (Ps. 8:5)?

Dimensions of Meaning

Title

Psalm 8 has something that Psalm 1 does not but that most other
psalms do—a title, which is not an actual part of the poem and is
probably an addition made at some point by the editors of the
book of Psalms. "To the leader" (see NIV, "For the director of
music") probably indicates that the Psalms were originally sung in
the temple, and later in the synagogues. According to 1 Chronicles 15:16–24 and 16:4–7, King David appointed Levitical musi-

cians even before the temple existed. This account is followed in
1 Chronicles 16:23–33 by words very similar to Psalm 96. To be
sure, the books of Chronicles are a relatively late creation, but
even if their account of David's work is not historically accurate,
the account itself is solid evidence for the singing of the Psalms in
Israelite and Judean worship.

We do not know what the singing of the Psalms sounded like
in ancient Israel and Judah, although one scholar, Suzanne Haïk
Vantoura, claims to have deciphered the ancient musical annotations and to have reconstructed the original melodies of the
Psalms.[2] Whether or not she is correct, it is clear that the
Psalms have been sung for thousands of years by Jews and
Christians, and that they continue to be sung in a variety of
ways, including Gregorian and Anglican chant, metrical
psalmody (the distinctive contribution of the Reformed tradition), responsorial versions, and more. Indeed, the last thirty
years have seen a revival of psalm-singing, and several recent
denominational hymnals include sections especially devoted to
the singing of the Psalms.

The meaning of the next phrase in the title, "according to the
Gittith," is unclear, as suggested by the fact that the NRSV has
transliterated, rather than translated, the Hebrew. The word
"Gittith" may indicate a musical instrument (see JPS, "on the gittith"), or it may be the name of an ancient melody. The final
phrase associates Psalm 8 with David, as is the case with seventy-
three psalms. This has traditionally been understood to indicate
Davidic authorship, but few contemporary scholars think that
David wrote any of the psalms. The Hebrew phrase in question—
more literally "to David"—could mean "written by David," but it
could also mean something like "in memory of David" or "dedicated to David." These latter proposals are more likely, historically speaking. In any case, the question of the authorship of the
Psalms, while interesting, is relatively unimportant. More important are the content and theology of the Psalms, or as suggested
above in our consideration of Psalm 1, what the Psalms teach us
about God, humankind, and the life of faith. In this regard, Psalm
8 has a great deal to offer.

Verses 1a, 9

The most obvious stylistic feature of Psalm 8 is that the opening and closing lines are identical. The very first word of the poem is the Hebrew personal name for God, YHWH. Because this name is so sacred, the practice among Jews has been not to pronounce it, but rather to substitute a Hebrew noun that means "Lord," which happens to be the second word of Psalm 8. This led to the RSV's "O LORD, our Lord," which the NRSV changed to "O LORD, our Sovereign." In any case, the focus at the boundaries of Psalm 8 is clearly on God and God's lordship or sovereignty over the whole creation—"all the earth." The adjective "majestic" is a word that elsewhere is used to described royal figures, thus further highlighting the emphasis on God's sovereignty as the psalm begins and ends. We shall return to a further consideration of verse 9 and the significance of the repetition that forms an envelope structure for the psalm.

Verses 1b–2

The focus remains on God, and the word "glory" reinforces the emphasis on God's sovereignty. But other characters are also introduced in this section—the "babes and infants," as well as God's "foes," "the enemy and the avenger." The RSV suggests that babies and infants recognize God's lordship by chanting glory to God. This is a possible construal, but John Goldingay suggests a different interpretive direction. Noting that babies and children are often mentioned in the Old Testament as victims of violence, Goldingay concludes:

> The cry of children [as victims] is a dominant note in history, and this reference to their cry suggests that in creating the world Yhwh was aware that this would be so and was taking action to ensure that the forces of violence could not always do as they wished to babies and sucklings. Yhwh's might and majesty were asserted and/or acknowledged at the beginning in anticipatory recognition that this would be important for the vulnerable.[3]

Certainty is elusive, but another possible direction of meaning is suggested by the NRSV, which associates the babies and infants with God's establishment of strength (NRSV, "a bulwark"). In short, God's first line of defense against God's "foes" is a bunch of babies! This may seem quite unlikely, but as a striking poetic hyperbole, this remarkable image anticipates very well the unlikely scenario to follow—that is, the weak and vulnerable human creature will be the royal agent of God's sovereignty by virtue of the gift of "dominion" (v. 6). In any case, for further reflection upon God's sovereignty, it is crucial to note both that God *has* enemies (see the chapters on Pss. 1 and 13) and that God chooses to share God's "dominion" or power.

Verses 3–4

Verse 3 begins with the only time in Psalm 8 that a human being is the subject of an active verb, and in this case, the action is rather passive—"When I look." The original and fundamental actor is still God, who "established" all the things the psalmist looks at in the panoramic view of the night sky. Given the vastness of the cosmos and the overwhelming majesty of God's creation, the psalmist is struck by the smallness and seeming insignificance of the human creature. The Hebrew noun translated "human being" in verse 4a is especially suggestive of human weakness, and the phrase translated "mortals" in verse 4b is more literally "son of a human" or "child of Adam,"[4] perhaps recalling the poor performance of the original humans in the opening chapters of the book of Genesis, which is clearly alluded to in verses 5–8. In any case, it is precisely the psalmist's perception of smallness, insignificance, and vulnerability that leads to the question in verse 4.

Verse 4 is exactly the middle poetic line of Psalm 8, at least according to the layout by the editors of *Biblia Hebraica Stuttgartensia*, the standard scholarly text of the Old Testament. Thus, the question in verse 4 is central, and it is central both structurally and theologically. Although not recognizable in English translations, the interrogative "what" in verse 4 represents the same Hebrew word as the exclamatory particle "how" in verses 1a and 9. Thus, the poet has quite intentionally drawn the reader's eye and mind to both the boundaries and the center of Psalm 8. Given God's overarching sovereignty (vv. 1a, 9), what is to be said of human identity and vocation (v. 4)? Verses 5–8 will offer a startlingly exalted view of the tiny and vulnerable human creature.

Verses 5–8

The boundaries of Psalm 8 (vv. 1a, 9) effectively feature and highlight God's sovereignty. As it turns out, the interior of the poem applies the language and attributes of sovereignty to the human being. The royal language is most obvious in verse 5b— "crowned," along with "glory" and "honor," words elsewhere used in conjunction with monarchs (the underlying Hebrew of the two occurrences of "glory" in vv. 1b and 5b is different, but the words are nearly synonymous, and both are used regularly in royal contexts). In short, the seemingly weak and insignificant human creature gets royal treatment from God!

To be sure, verse 5a has already suggested the exalted status of humankind in God's sight. The NRSV's "little lower than God" is probably the best translation, although the phrase is ambiguous. The Hebrew noun translated "God" is a plural noun, explaining the NIV's "little lower than the heavenly beings" (see also KJV's "little less than the angels"). But this plural noun is regularly used in the Old Testament with the singular sense of "God," so the NRSV is certainly defensible, and it has the advantage of reminding the reader that the psalm employs royal terminology in describing both God and humankind. Given the clear allusions to Genesis 1 in verses 6–8, it is somewhat surprising that the psalmist does not use the phrase "image of God" (see Gen. 1:27), but verse 5 seems to be a poetic way of communicating what the phrase "image of God" suggests in Genesis.

In any case, just as "image of God" in Genesis 1:27 is followed by God's granting of "dominion" (Gen. 1:28) to humanity, so the articulation of humanity's exalted status in Psalm 8:5 is followed by the recognition that God has "given them dominion over" God's "works" (see "works" also in v. 3; the Hebrew words underlying "dominion" differ in Ps. 8:5 and Gen. 1:28, but they are clearly synonymous). The list in verses 7–8 clearly recalls Genesis 1:28, although the two passages are by no means identical. A frequently asked question is whether Psalm 8 is based in part on Genesis 1, or whether perhaps Genesis 1 is a fuller account of creation based in part on Psalm 8. The answer to this question is unclear, since the dating of the Psalms is so elusive. In any case, there is clearly a relationship between the two texts that cannot be ignored.

Verse 9: A Reprise

As we have seen, verse 9 is identical to verse 1a, providing an envelope structure for the psalm, but scholars of language and literature often point out that there is no such thing as exact repetition. In this case, for instance, even though verses 1a and 9 are exactly the same, letter for letter, readers will hear verse 9 differently than they heard verse 1, because of the intervening material in verses 1b–8, especially verses 4–8. In particular, by verse 9 the reader realizes that God's majestic sovereignty "in all the earth" is bound up with humanity and its exercise of the "dominion" God has granted. A stylistic key toward recognizing the different meaning that verse 9 has in its position following verses 4–8 is the repetition of the word "all."[5] It occurs in verses 1a and 9, where perhaps it is more obvious than its two occurrences in verses 6 and 7. Verse 6 is especially comprehensive in affirming that God has "put all things under their feet," and this means that the perception of God's majesty "in all the earth" will inevitably be affected by what humanity does with "all things under their feet." In other words, if humanity performs poorly in its exercise of "dominion," then God's "name," or we might say, God's *reputation*, will not look so good "in all the earth." This conclusion has remarkable implications for the appropriation of Psalm 8, including ones that are tremendously important for today.

Psalm 8 for Today

We have considered the careful poetic structuring of Psalm 8 that highlights the boundaries of the poem (vv. 1a, 9) and its center (v.

4). Walter Brueggemann has suggested that the key issue in hearing and responding faithfully to the message of Psalm 8 involves holding the center and the boundaries in proper interpretive balance.[6] If, for instance, one focuses too exclusively on verses 1a and 9, one is apt to overemphasize God's sovereignty and not pay sufficient attention to verse 4 and the centrality of humankind and human sovereignty in God's creative design. The danger associated with this imbalance will be that we human beings will not recognize and exercise the "dominion" God has given us. In essence, the danger is that we become lazy or passive, waiting for God to do what God has called us to do in the world, or perhaps counting on God to "fix" the messes that we make of things in the world.

In our contemporary setting, this danger may be less likely than the danger of overemphasizing verse 4 and not paying sufficient attention to verses 1a and 9. In other words, we contemporary folk seem all too ready to accept the centrality of humankind and to exercise our "dominion" or power. The crucial question for us is this: Will we recognize any limits or boundaries to our power? Or, in terms of the poetic structure of Psalm 8, will we recognize that human sovereignty (vv. 3–8, including the central v. 4) is surrounded, bounded, and delimited by God's sovereignty? If we do not recognize that our sovereignty is to be bounded and delimited by God's prior claim on us and our world, if we do not recognize that our power is a God-given gift rather than a right, then our exercise of dominion will inevitably become the practice of domination and a prelude to disaster.

Indeed, some observers are saying that this is precisely what is happening today, and they point to creation or nature and the ominous and potentially catastrophic conditions that we human beings have produced: the pollution of the earth's air and water, with consequences such as the rapidly increased rate of the disappearance of plant and animal species, and the precipitous rise in the earth's temperature. We have recently heard a great deal about "global warming" and "climate change," and we will undoubtedly be hearing more and more in the months and years ahead as episodes of extreme weather increase, as the water level in Lake

Superior continues to drop, as tidal marshes and coastal wetlands continue to be threatened and lost, as rain forests disappear, as glaciers and polar ice caps continue to melt, as nations vie for control of the newly accessible (due to melting ice) "Northwest Passage" connecting the Atlantic and Pacific Oceans, as polar bears are threatened with extinction because their frozen habitat is melting, and so on. Of course, there is also the threat, due again to global warming and the melting of polar ice, of a dramatic rise in sea level throughout the world, possibly as much as twenty feet, in which case there would be catastrophic consequences, as the oceans would claim land on which hundreds of millions of people now reside. The experts suggest that time is quickly running out, but that it is not too late to reverse the current trends and perhaps to avoid at least the most catastrophic consequences of global warming. Meanwhile, in the midst of this environmental crisis, Psalm 8 invites us to consider that from a biblical perspective, ecology and theology are inseparable. In other words, confronting and dealing constructively with today's ecological crisis is not only a matter of science and technology, but it is also a matter of faithfulness to God and God's purposes for the world. As James Limburg concludes, "In these times of ecological crisis, Psalm 8 is a call for humans to act as responsible royalty and to care for the fragile blue planet we call our home."[7]

Clearly at issue is this: What constitutes the faithful exercise of dominion? Or to put it in slightly different but still biblical terms, what does it mean to image God? These are large and fundamentally important theological questions, which involve both how we understand God and how we understand ourselves as human beings. To be sure, we will not in these pages be able to say all that could be said in addressing these big questions, but we can make a solid start. As for a biblical perspective on what it means to exercise dominion faithfully, Psalm 8 itself is a good starting point. In Psalm 8, God exercises power *by sharing it.* In short, power is not the unilateral exertion of authority or force to benefit oneself and to pursue one's own agenda; rather, it inherently involves sharing. And to bring the opening chapters of Genesis into the picture, the faithful exercise of dominion should have the effect of preserving the entire creation, which God repeatedly pronounces "good" (Gen. 1:4, 10, 12, 18, 21, 25, 31—note that the total is seven, the biblical number for wholeness or completeness, and that the seventh occurrence is "very good"). Anything that violates or destroys the goodness of "everything that he [God] had made" (Gen. 1:31) is not a faithful exercise of dominion. This conclusion is reinforced by the vocation of the original humans in the garden in Genesis 2:15—"to serve and preserve it" (my translation; NRSV, "to till and keep it"). In other words, the faithful exercise of dominion involves not only sharing but also caring. Again, to endanger or destroy the earth and its creatures is domination, not faithfully exercised dominion.

This conclusion is reinforced even further by the larger canonical witness, which turns out to be a massive and persuasive project to portray sovereignty not in terms of force and enforcement, but rather in terms of love. Again, the direction of Psalm 8 is determinative. God exercises God's power by *giving it away*. According to Douglas John Hall, "This is the great risk taken by the biblical God."[8] But it is precisely this risk that makes love possible. If human beings were not free, if we were programmed to obey, then genuine relatedness—that is, love—would not be possible. In Hall's words, "A being programmed to love would be no lover."[9] Of course, what makes love possible is also what makes disobedience possible—thus God's "great risk." God wills us to obey, to love, to exercise dominion faithfully as sharing and caring, for God's sake and for the sake of all creation. Sometimes we do, but often we do not. To be sure, disobedience always produces destructive consequences, but rather than simply enforcing the divine will by punishing humankind, God forgives, bearing the burden of human sinfulness so that the relationship will be maintained. Such grace, such self-giving love, is the character of God's sovereignty. This is the way that God exercises power, and God invites us to do likewise.

So the faithful exercise of human sovereignty—"dominion," or power—is to be characterized by love, not force. The Judean king, who was viewed as the human agent of God's will, even to the point of being seen as the "son of God" (see Ps. 2:6–7; 2 Sam.

7:14), was supposed to exercise his power and authority on behalf of others, particularly the poor, weak, and needy (see Ps. 72, especially vv. 1–7, 12–14). Because of the ceremony that took place when a king was crowned, kings were known as God's "anointed" (Ps. 2:2), a translation of Hebrew *messiah*, the Greek of which is *christos*. From the Christian perspective, Jesus *Christ* is the fullest and most complete expression of genuine royalty, and, of course, Jesus exercised power or sovereignty not as enforcement but as self-giving love.

In the process, Jesus demonstrated as well that true royalty and suffering are not mutually exclusive. At this point, the canonical placement of Psalm 8 is relevant. In short, the suffering represented and articulated in Psalms 3–7—opposition, weakness, distress, grief—does not stand in contradiction to the exalted status of humanity in Psalm 8. Or, in other biblical terms, to suffer is not a contradiction of what it means to image God. This conclusion is extraordinary! Not only does it help us human beings to accept finitude and fallibility as part of our identity, including the suffering that necessarily follows (see the chapter on Ps. 13), but it also suggests that God suffers too, a reality that we Christians see expressed quintessentially in the cross of Jesus Christ. Putting all this together, to live out the royal identity that God has bestowed upon us (Ps. 8:5–8) means to image God by the practice of dominion as self-giving love, a vocation that means inevitably we will suffer for the sake of others, just as God is willing to do and, in fact, does.

The issue of suffering and human identity is explored thoroughly in the book of Job, and it is not surprising that there is a clear intertextual connection between Psalm 8:4 and Job 7:17. In effect, Job 7:17–18 reverses the perspective of Psalm 8:4–5—that is, Job's abysmal suffering leads him to deny the goodness of life, and Job cannot reconcile the experience of suffering with the royal status of humankind. But by the end of the book, Job has rediscovered his desire to live, expressing his newly found vitality in royal terms (see Job 31:35–37; compare Ps. 8:5). And when God finally answers the challenge Job has issued in 31:35–37, the divine speeches (chapters 38–41) are creation-oriented, like Psalms 8 and

Genesis 1. While these speeches have traditionally been understood as God's attempt to humiliate Job and to put him in his place, they should be understood as God's attempt to challenge Job, in the midst of his suffering, to step up and claim the royal vocation of dominion God intends for the human creature. Unfortunately, the NRSV offers a translation of Job 42:6, the conclusion of Job's reply to God, that reflects this traditional misunderstanding:

> therefore I despise myself,
> and repent in dust and ashes.

A better translation of Job 42:6 is this by Gerald Janzen:

> therefore I recant [that is, Job takes back the sorts of things he said in 7:17–18],
> and change my mind about dust and ashes [that is, Job has a new view of the character and vocation of the weak and vulnerable human creature].[10]

What Job has learned, and thus changes his mind about, is that human suffering is not incompatible with imaging God, and thus that God suffers too, as a result of God's loving investment in and involvement with the world. This is an extraordinarily important conclusion, one that is suggested as well by the juxtaposition of Psalms 3–7 with Psalm 8, and one that resonates clearly with the New Testament.

It is to be especially noted and emphasized that the above discussion of Psalm 8 has focused on the identity and vocation of *humanity*. It is not Israel or Judah or "the righteous" whom God has "crowned . . . with glory and honor" (v. 5). It is humanity! Noting this fact, and reading Psalm 8 in the context of the book of Psalms and the larger canon, James L. Mays refers to humankind as "God's *anthropos* [Greek for "humanity"] project," and he points out that the effect of Psalm 8 and the book of Psalms is to "support a vision of the meaning and worth of the human being."[11] Mays's elaboration upon the direction of this vision articulates its tremendous importance for today:

Philosophical anthropologists point out that, historically, human beings have sought their identity by comparing themselves to animals, to others, and to God. Only the second is absent from the psalm [Psalm 8]. Here the human is not known by comparison to other races, nations, cultures. The omission is not accidental, and its absence must be emphasized. The notion of universal humankind has been around for a long time, but the drift of history does not favor it. Tribalism, nationalism, racism—all the ways of being human in distinction from others and in hostility to others—govern the self-consciousness of the majority of the species. In every crisis of culture and at every transition in history, we have to learn again how to say "human being." By any other language, we do not discover but destroy ourselves. And in that fact alone, the left hand of the God of the universe shepherds us toward the realization of universal *ben-adam* [literally, "child of humanity" = humankind; see Ps. 8:4].[12]

The affirmation that God wills nothing short of a "universal *ben-adam*" means, as Mays suggests, that God values, cares for, and loves *every* human being. To be sure, this affirmation is hard to believe, and in fact, almost no one seems to believe it. But as Mays rightly recognizes, to fail to believe it means to invite disaster and destruction. In a world where racism is still rampant, where narrow nationalism seems to be on the increase, and where tensions between and among ethnic and religious groups regularly erupt into hostility and war, it is crucial to affirm that God loves the whole creation, including every human being. Indeed, God loves humanity so much that God has entrusted this majestic creation to our care, risking God's own reputation, and perhaps the future of the creation itself, for love's sake. In the final analysis, then, Psalm 8 invites us in return to love God, to love each other, and to love the world that God has established. In the words of a familiar hymn, the love God has shown to us human beings, as well as the trust God has placed in us, demands "our soul, our life, our all." Such submission is the essence of praise.

Questions for Reflection and Discussion

1. Despite the fact that the cross is the central symbol of the Christian faith, many Christians seem never to have thought seriously about God's suffering. What is the significance of God's "great risk" in sharing "dominion" with humanity? Besides opening God to disappointment and suffering, what other consequences may there be for God as a result of the decision to share power with humankind?
2. It is helpful to think about praise not only as a liturgical activity but also as a way of life. What are some possible points of contact between praise as a way of living and what Psalm 1:6 commends as the "way of the righteous"?
3. Recall the conclusion in this chapter that Psalm 8 suggests the inseparability of theology and ecology. Consider global warming as one aspect of the "ecological crisis" mentioned by Limburg. How do you think Psalm 8 speaks to the crisis? What can you do in response? See the list of "51 Things You Can Do to Make a Difference" in *Time*, April 9, 2007, 69–100 (available online at http://www.time .com/time/specials/2007/environment) for ideas.
4. Why do you think it is important for today that, as Mays suggests, humankind is God's "*anthropos* project" and that God "shepherds us toward the realization of universal *ben-adam*"?
5. Some philosophical anthropologists suggest that as individuals and groups, we human beings seek status and meaning only over against others—in Mays's words, we seek to be "human in distinction from others and in hostility to others." If Psalm 8, the book of Psalms, and the Bible as a whole invite a different way to be human, how do we resist the temptations toward tribalism, nationalism, and racism in pursuit of a more excellent way?

Chapter Three

Psalm 13

I n the space of only six verses, Psalm 13 exemplifies admirably what the prayers in the book of Psalms are all about. As James L. Mays puts it, "Though it is the shortest of the prayers of salvation in the Book of Psalms, it comprehends their essential elements so completely that to know it is to have an introduction to the others."[1] Thus, Psalm 13 proves to be an excellent choice for a volume such as this, in which we can cover only a small selection of the Psalms. In our treatment of Psalm 13, we shall depend upon it to put us in touch with the issues that are raised generally by the prayers in the Psalter.

One issue involves what to call the prayers. Mays calls them "prayers for salvation" or "prayers for help." This may be the most accurate description of them; however, these prayers have traditionally been known among scholars as "laments of an individual," or "complaints," or "protests." These labels capture well the content found in Psalm 13:1–2, whereas the designation "prayers for help" picks up more clearly the content of Psalm 13:3–4. In any case, although the book of Psalms in Hebrew is called "Praises," these prayers actually are represented more often than the hymns or songs of praise (see Pss. 8, 103, 148). Of course, as Psalm 13:5–6 demonstrates, praise is not absent from the prayers.

Each of the three two-verse sections of Psalm 13 contains one of the essential elements of the prayers for help. Verses 1–2 are the lament, complaint, or protest proper, and this section contains a description of the psalmist's problem. Even so, it has proven very difficult to determine exactly what the psalmist's problem(s) may have been in any given prayer. In the case of Psalm 13, for instance, commentators often suggest that the psalmist was ill. This is a reasonable conclusion, but it is by no means necessary. Here and in the other prayers, the language and imagery are general and stereotypical enough to suggest a variety of possible problems or afflictions. What is clear, of course, is that something is desperately and urgently wrong, and that the psalmist needs help.

Even though the psalmists have been told by their opponents that "there is no help for you in God" (Ps. 3:2), the psalmists never believe this. As severe as their afflictions seem to be, and as much as they may seem to blame God in an accusatory and even blasphemous-sounding way, the psalmists always look to God for help. So the prayers generally move from a description of the problems(s) to a plea for help. Whereas this movement seems logical enough, it is the final element of Psalm 13 (vv. 5–6) and the other prayers for help that seems surprising. This element has traditionally been known among scholars as "the certainty of being heard," and because there seems to be no preparation for the shift to trust and praise and joy, as well as because this shift does not seem to fit very well with the lament/complaint and plea, this element of the prayers has been the subject of a great deal of scholarly discussion and debate. We shall explore some of the interpretive possibilities later, but for now, suffice it to say that all the individual prayers for help include this element, except for Psalm 88.

In addition to the typical elements of the prayers for help, the prayers regularly feature the same cast of characters—that is, the psalmist(s), God, and the opponents of the psalmist(s). The latter are often called, as in Psalm 13:2, the "enemy," but they also go under a host of other designations: "foe," "adversary," "oppressor," "wicked," and so on. It is crucial to note and to take seriously how this cast of characters is described, because the interpretive implications are profoundly important theologically. For instance, there is no question that the psalmists always appeal to and have confidence in God and God's ability to help. In short, they view God as sovereign, as do the songs of praise (see the chapter on Ps. 8). At the same time, however, God and the psalmists always have enemies. What does this say about God and about how God exercises sovereignty or power? The pervasive presence of enemies means too that the psalmists always have problems—hence the cogency of labeling the prayers as laments, complaints, or protests. What Jewish writer Isaac Bashevis Singer said one time about himself aptly captures the situation of the psalmists: "I only pray when I'm in trouble, but I'm in trouble all the time."[2] Of what significance is it that the psalmists, who constitute the faithful, or "the righteous" (see the chapter on Ps. 1), are constantly suffering?

These large and important questions mean that the prayers for help will be instructive not only as biblical models for prayer but also in terms of how we understand God, ourselves, and the life of faith. Let us keep these questions in mind as we consider Psalm 13 in more detail and as we consider its significance for today.

Dimensions of Meaning

Verses 1–2

We have seen that repetition is an important stylistic device in Hebrew poetry, including the Psalms, and the most noticeable literary feature of verses 1–2 is the fourfold repetition of "How long?" The phrase is obviously an interrogative, meaning that the initial tone of Psalm 13 is one of questioning, or perhaps even doubt. To be sure, the apparent doubt will not turn out to be total doubt, since God will be addressed as "my God" in verse 3, and then too, of course, there is the "trust" of verse 5. But it is instructive that faith and doubt, trust and questioning, are juxtaposed here. Perhaps they are not as antithetical as we often suppose.

The effect of the repetition is to draw out the lament or

complaint, thus heightening the sense of impatience, desperation, and urgency. Adding to the intensity of the situation is the fact that with each "How long?" the description of the trouble gets increasingly worse. In the first instance, the psalmist asks about having been forgotten, but then the matter becomes that God has hidden God's face. The third "How long?" articulates the debilitating effects of the situation. As the NRSV note suggests, "bear pain in my soul" is a translation of the Syriac version of the Old Testament. The Hebrew, "hold counsels," may suggest just as clearly the inner turmoil of the psalmist, as he or she can get no rest because of turning things over and over again in the mind and heart. The sorrow is pervasive; the trouble lasts "all day long." The fourth and climactic "How long?" shifts the focus outward with the mention of the enemy. Elsewhere in the Psalms, God is known as the "Exalted One," but here the "enemy . . . [is] exalted over me." It is as if to say that the enemy seems to have displaced God—a worst-case scenario. As Robert Alter sums up the movement of verses 1–2, the "series of four times 'how long' . . . reflects an ascent on a scale of intensity, the note of urgency pitched slightly higher with each repetition."[3]

Erhard Gerstenberger suggests that the questions voiced by the psalmist in verses 1–2 are "rather impertinent."[4] Perhaps they are, but such impertinence is not unusual in the prayers for help. Just as I suggested above that questioning and trust are not necessarily antithetical, I suggest here that the psalmist's impertinence is not an indiction of a lack of faith. To put it more positively perhaps, the psalmist is being completely honest with God. The good news is that such honesty is apparently what God expects in prayer, even when it may take the form of desperate impatience or even impertinence.

As we have seen, the precise nature of the trouble is unclear. Similarly, it is not clear who or what the enemies are, or exactly what they may be doing or may have done to the psalmist. This lack of specificity in Psalm 13 and the other prayers for help suggests the appropriateness of interpreting symbolically the enemies in the Psalms. As Mays puts it:

The enemies are out to deprive the afflicted of either shalom or *sedaqah* [usually translated "righteousness"—that is, the condition of things being right] or both. That is what makes them theologically important and what makes them a symbol that can be used in other and quite different social and cultural settings from the ones in which they were written. . . . We pray because we desire that God's will and mind prevail— not our own, not others'.[5]

Ultimately, the psalmists' prayers express the urgent, fervent desire that they experience the fullness of life—shalom and "righteousness"—that God wills for humankind.

Verses 3–4

The grammatical shift from interrogatives to imperatives marks the transition from the lament-complaint-protest proper in verses 1–2 to the plea for help in verses 3–4—"consider," "answer," and "give light." The three imperatives are accompanied by three reasons that God should act, and again, the urgency of the situation is evident. Indeed, it is a matter of life and death. The juxtaposition of "death" (v. 3) and "my enemy" (v. 4) leads some commentators to conclude that the enemy is death. A symbolic interpretation would permit such a conclusion, but it is by no means necessary. The plural "foes" actually seems to indicate human opponents who may have contributed to the psalmist's desperate situation but who, in any case, rejoice at the psalmist's misfortune and seemingly imminent demise.

Verses 5–6

This final section of Psalm 13 seems surprising and unexpected. The expressions of trust, joy, and praise do not seem to fit with the desperate lament of verses 1–2 and the urgent pleas of verses 3–4. But, literarily speaking, there are several indications of unity between verses 1–4 and 5–6. In particular, three words or phrases from verses 1–4 recur in verses 5–6, and this pattern of repetition serves to sharpen even further the contrast. The first instance is "heart." In verse 2, the psalmist complains of "sorrow in my heart all day long," but in verse 5, "my heart rejoices in your salvation" (NIV). The second case of repetition is "rejoices(s)." Whereas the psalmist fears in verse 4 that "my foes will rejoice," it is the same psalmist in verse 5 whose "heart rejoices" in God's gift of salvation—that is, God's life-giving help. The third instance of repetition involves the identical Hebrew phrase translated "over me" in verse 2 and "with me" in verse 6. Whereas the psalmist saw the enemy "exalted over me" in verse 2, the psalmist celebrates in verse 6 that God "has dealt bounty over me" (my translation).

These three cases of repetition signal emphatically that something is quite different in verses 5–6. But what? And how, or why? One major interpretive option is to conclude that the psalmist's prayer for help has been answered—that is, the illness has been cured (if indeed this had been the problem), or the enemies have been disposed of, so that God seems present again. In this case, however, one must assume a passage of time between verses 4 and 5, perhaps a long time. To be sure, this is possible, but a major problem with this conclusion is that there is no textual support for it in (or beyond) the psalm. A more serious problem is the implication that joy and praise are possible only beyond distress and suffering, and that God is only perceptibly present when things are going well. Neither of these directions is supported by the book of Psalms or by the Bible as a whole.

Fortunately, there are other and more helpful interpretive options. The traditional scholarly option proposes that after the psalmist prayed verses 1–4 in the temple, a priest delivered a promise of God's help, but this promise has not been included in the text. Rather, according to this proposal, the psalmist's response to the priestly promise is found in verses 5–6. What had changed was not the physical circumstances or conditions of the psalmist but rather the psalmist himself or herself, or at least the psalmist's attitude or outlook on things. In essence, the psalmist had entrusted life and future to God, and joyfully and praisefully ("I will sing to the LORD," v. 6) awaited God's help.

Of course, this scholarly approach suffers from the same major problem as above—namely, there is no textual support for it in (or beyond) the psalm. Nonetheless, it is probably on the right track, at least insofar as it suggests that verses 5–6 do not assume changed conditions or circumstances from those described in verses 1–4, and that any change which has occurred is in the psalmist's own self. In this sense, the traditional scholarly approach has some affinity with what I judge to be a more satisfactory and less speculative attempt to account for the apparent inconsistency between verses 1–4 and verses 5–6. This final approach does not attempt to discover what happened between verses 4 and 5. Rather, it is a more literary or canonical approach that takes seriously the juxtaposition between verses 1–4 and verses 5–6, and in which the apparent inconsistency is actually the primary interpretive clue. This approach is articulated eloquently by James L. Mays in his exposition of Psalm 13:

> There is a powerful testimony to God in what seems a serious inconsistency in the prayer. . . . Luther in his exposition of the Psalm calls the mood of the prayer the "state in which hope despairs, and yet despair hopes at the same time." . . .
>
> There is a coherence which holds the apparently separate moments together. God is so much a god of blessing and salvation for the psalmist that he must speak of tribulation and terror as the absence of God. Yet God is so much the God of *hesed* ["steadfast love," v. 5] for the psalmist that he can speak to God in the midst of tribulation and terror as the God of his salvation. This is the deep radical knowledge of faith which cannot separate God from any experience of life and perseveres in construing all, including life's worst, in terms of a relation to God. It is the expression of such a powerful experience of graciousness that it refuses to see the present apart from God and cannot imagine the future apart from his salvation. . . . Plaint and praise alike are the triumph of grace.
> . . . The Psalm is not given us to use on the rare occasions when some trouble seems to make it appropriate. It is forever appropriate as long as life shall last. We do not begin at

one end and come out at the other. The agony and the
ecstasy belong together as the secret of our identity.[6]

Note well the *simultaneity* and the *inseparability* of agony and
ecstasy, pain and praise, suffering and glory in human life, including the life of the faithful. This reality has profound theological
significance for today and for all seasons.

Psalm 13 for Today

According to clinical psychologist Mary Pipher, our culture does
not handle suffering very well. In fact, Pipher contends "that
almost all the craziness in the world comes from running from
pain."[7] What we need to teach and learn in our culture, Pipher
says, is that pain and suffering are inevitable realities of human
life. So often, however, we are told just the opposite, as she points
out in the following:

> I recently saw a book written for "adults hurt as children."
> This title sends the odd message that there are adults who
> were not hurt as children. In fact, all humans are fallible and
> all parents err. When we suggest that suffering can be
> avoided, we foster unreasonable expectations. We are send-
> ing the same message that advertisers send. Advertisers
> imply that suffering is unnatural, shouldn't be tolerated and
> can be avoided with the right products. Psychologists some-
> times imply that stress-free living is possible if only we have
> the right tools. But in fact, all our stories have sad endings.
> We all die in the last act.[8]

Although Pipher is a psychologist, her insights at this point are
profoundly biblical and theological. We are sinful creatures—"all
humans are fallible," as she puts it. Moreover, we are finite—"we
all die in the last act." This means that suffering simply *will be* a
part of human life, no matter how much we might try to deny it
or avoid it. This lesson is one that Psalm 13 and the other prayers
for help could teach us. As Mays puts it, "I wonder if we could not

use this poetry of human desperation to discern our true and authentic neediness."[9]

Indeed, we could! The question is, Will we? The church in recent years has not felt comfortable with the prayers for help; consequently, the church has not used them very frequently. This loss, as Walter Brueggemann suggests, is "costly." In congruence with Pipher, Brueggemann points out that the first cost of losing the laments is psychological. If we think that suffering and need-iness are not normal, we will regularly engage in denial and avoid-ance, often pretending that things are all right with us and the world, even when things are clearly not right. The result is our creation of "false selves," and this leads to the second cost, which is sociological. That is to say, "false selves" engaged in denial and avoidance will be incapable of forming and participating in gen-uine community (see the chapter on Ps. 1). The third cost, accord-ing to Brueggemann, is theological. By failing to acknowledge, confront, and articulate our own pain and the pain of the world, we misunderstand who God is and where and how God is at work in the world.[10]

There are far too many Christians who view God as a sort of cosmic scorekeeper, handing out rewards and punishments according to what each person deserves. In this theological sys-tem, suffering logically means that a person must have done something wrong, and that God is against him or her. At this point, it is crucial to take seriously that it is *the righteous* who pray the prayers in the book of Psalms. Even when they suggest that they may deserve punishment and that God may be punishing them (see the chapters on Pss. 32 and 51), they ultimately con-clude that God is with them and for them. In many of the prayers for help, it is clear that the psalmists are suffering precisely as a result of their faithfulness. In this case, it is not God who is caus-ing their suffering; rather, the enemies, who oppose God and God's purposes, are the cause. In short, the psalmists are suffering not because they have been bad but because they have been good!

It is not surprising, therefore, that the prophet Jeremiah, who suffered severely as a result of his faithful proclamation of God's word, prayed prayers very much like the laments in the book of

Psalms (see Jer. 11:18–12:6; 15:10–21; 17:14–18; 18:18–23; 20:7–13). And it is crucial to note that the Gospel writers could not relate the story of Jesus' suffering and death without frequent recourse to the prayers for help, especially Psalms 22, 31, and 69, the three longest and most intense of the laments. In Matthew and Mark, Jesus' prayer from the cross is the opening line of Psalm 22, "My God, my God, why have you forsaken me?" Not only does Jesus' use of Psalm 22 from the cross serve to legitimate the psalmic prayers as fundamental biblical models for prayer, but it also reinforces the conclusion that the psalmists, like Jesus, suffered not because they were bad but because they were faithful and good.

The cumulative effect of all this—that is, the prayers for help in the book of Psalms, as well as echoes of them in the book of Jeremiah and their use in the passion narratives in the Gospels—is simply to obliterate the doctrine of retribution, including its simplistic moral calculus that construes suffering as divine punishment and as evidence of alienation from God. To the contrary, we could and should learn from the prayers for help—in Mays's words, to "discern our true and authentic neediness" as fallible, finite human beings. In our culture of denial and avoidance of pain at all costs, the prayers for help could and should help us to avoid instead, in Pipher's words, "the craziness [that] . . . comes from running from pain."

But there is more. The prayers for help can teach us not only that suffering is an inevitable human experience but also that suffering is to be anticipated, and even embraced, as part of the life of faith. In the Gospel of Mark, Jesus' most direct invitation to discipleship is this: "If any want to become my followers, let them deny themselves and take up their cross and follow me" (Mark 8:34). To follow Jesus will mean to suffer more, not less. This does not mean that suffering is good, nor that it is to be enjoyed, nor that it is inherently redemptive. Even Jesus, anticipating the cross, prayed that God might "remove this cup from me" (Mark 14:36). Suffering that results from or perpetuates injustice is to be steadfastly resisted and opposed, as Jesus' ministry demonstrates. What is good, and what is to be enjoyed, and what is inherently redemptive is love, but to love and to be lovingly involved in a world of finite, fallible human beings will inevitably mean to suffer. Suffering for love's sake is what Jesus taught and embodied, and as his followers we can anticipate and embrace such suffering, entrusting our lives and futures to God, as Jesus and the psalmists always did. For us, as for the psalmists and the prophets and Jesus, the agony and the ecstasy will belong together as the secret of our identity. Or, to paraphrase Mays's conclusion in explicitly Christian terms, the cross and the resurrection will belong together as the secret of our identity.

In some quarters today, the church is having major difficulty affirming the simultaneity and inseparability of the agony and the ecstasy, the cross and the resurrection. The so-called prosperity gospel is alive and well in the United States and beyond; its appeal to rich and poor alike is that it promises a quick, material "fix." That is, if one believes fervently enough, God will make one rich. Those who have already "succeeded" can conveniently congratulate themselves for being so good, while the poor are lured by the promise of future "success." What the prosperity gospel misses, of course, is any discernment of the cross or costly discipleship. It reduces faith to something closely akin to the power of positive thinking, and it installs God in the position of cosmic scorekeeper, who is obligated to reward people materially for their faith and devotion. Needless to say, the prosperity gospel eventually leaves countless persons bitter and disillusioned when their "faith" does not pay off and when God alledgedly does not come through for them.

The prayers for help, along with the prophets and Jesus, expose the prosperity gospel for what it really is—a false promise that fosters bad faith. The prosperity or peace that God promises, according to Jesus, is not "as the world gives" (John 14:27). The prosperity gospel simply invites and encourages greed. In contrast, by obliterating the doctrine of retribution, the prayers for help in the book of Psalms, along with the cross, make grace a logical possibility. As we have seen, Mays suggests that Psalm 13 is "a powerful expression of graciousness," and that for the psalmist, "Plaint and praise alike are the triumph of grace." What grace invites and encourages is gratitude, which Reformed forebear John Calvin identified as the quintessential posture of discipleship. Thus, as Calvin also suggested, the psalms at this point effectively "teach and train us to bear the cross."[11] In so doing, we shall not only be faithful followers of Jesus, but we may also discover that we will avoid, and help others to avoid, "all the craziness in the world [that] comes from running from pain."

Questions for Reflection and Discussion

1. According to Mary Pipher, the "craziness" she mentions particularly affects young people in our culture. One of the results of not preparing young people to anticipate pain and suffering as a normal part of human life may be the extraordinarily high rates of suicide among young people. The rock group REM has a song entitled "Everybody Hurts" that addresses this issue and that has been used along with its video over the past several years in teen suicide-prevention campaigns. Quite appropriately, the video cites two lament psalms, Psalms 61 and 126. If possible, view the video (which is on the video collection entitled *Parallel* and is also available on YouTube). How may it be related to the prayers for help, and how may it help us to appreciate their message for today?

2. A universal human experience of suffering is the grief felt as a result of the loss of a loved one. One of my students recently completed a master's project entitled "Psalms as a Resource for Those Grieving the Loss of a Loved One," in which, among other things, she had participants study Psalm 13. She concluded in part that Psalm 13 "helps them [persons who have experienced the recent loss of a spouse] give voice to their grieving when words are sometimes hard to find" and that it "gives them permission to be honest with God."[12] How have prayers for help been useful to you in a time of loss? How could they be useful to you and others in the future?

3. A popular contemporary movement, which has a religious foundation, encourages people to try not to complain for twenty-one days, in an attempt to create "a complaint free world" (see http://www.acomplaintfreeworld.org and the book by Will Bowen, *A Complaint Free World: How to Stop Complaining and Start Enjoying the Life You Always Wanted*). To be sure, lots of people almost certainly do need to complain less and to be more satisfied with who they are and/or what they have. And to be fair to this movement, its Web site contains the following definition, attributed to Eckhart Tolle: "Complaining is not to be confused with informing someone of a mistake or deficiency so that it can be put right. And to refrain from complaining doesn't necessarily mean putting up with a bad quality or behavior." Even so, given the fact that the prayers for help in the Psalter are fundamental biblical models for prayer, and that they are often labeled "complaints," what are the possible dangers of not complaining? How might one make a distinction between legitimate complaints and ones that should be eliminated?

4. As Mays suggests, Psalm 13 is not just for "the rare occasions when some trouble seems to make it appropriate." To pray this psalm and similar prayers regularly is to be put in touch with our perpetual neediness, but a tradition of the ecumenical church is to pray the Psalms for others as well as for ourselves. How might Psalm 13 and the other prayers for help put us in touch with the pain and neediness of the world, and why is this important?

5. Given the assessment by Walter Brueggemann and others that lament has been largely lost in the contemporary church, how might we go about a process of recovery? Do you have specific ideas you could share with pastors and other leaders in your congregation?

Chapter Four

Psalm 23

Psalm 23 is undoubtedly the most familiar psalm in the book of Psalms, and it may be the most familiar passage in the entire Bible. So familiar is it, in fact, that William Holladay describes it as "an American secular icon."[1] As this description suggests, the familiarity of Psalm 23 is not limited to people of faith. On the one hand, the fact that Psalm 23 is so widely known is a good thing, especially in an era of growing biblical illiteracy. On the other hand, the "secularization" of Psalm 23 may make it more difficult to hear and appropriate its radical invitation to live a thoroughly God-centered life (see the chapter on Ps. 1). The exposition and reflections that follow will attempt to "de-secularize" Psalm 23 and thus enable us to begin to understand and to respond faithfully to its call to entrust life and future to God alone.

To be sure, the fact that Psalm 23 has become "an American secular icon" does not mean that it has failed to function effectively and powerfully among people of faith. Over the past twenty years of teaching and learning about the Psalms with church groups, I have often taken informal surveys by asking people to share with me their favorite psalm. The winner is always Psalm 23. It is known, it is loved, and it has often served and continues to serve as a powerful influence in the lives of the faithful, especially in situations of extremity and loss. It is largely in this capacity, of course, that Psalm 23 has gained its reputation as "a funeral psalm," as well as a psalm to be used by the bedside of desperately ill and dying persons. In these contexts, Psalm 23 has been and is a powerful presence, capable of providing comfort and assurance when perhaps no other words can.

More so than its familiarity, it is this ability of Psalm 23 to speak powerfully in situations of extremity and loss that Walter Brueggemann has in mind when he begins his commentary on Psalm 23 with the following words: "It is almost pretentious to comment on this psalm."[2] In other words, given the obvious and widely experienced ability of Psalm 23 to speak to people in distress, what more can be or need be said? Brueggemann is correct, and because this dimension of Psalm 23 really needs no comment, the treatment that follows will explore how Psalm 23 can be for us today something more than simply "a funeral psalm." It will explore how Psalm 23 can be for us a psalm for daily use, a psalm that is as much about life and living as it is about death and dying.

Psalm 23 is usually categorized by biblical scholars as a psalm of assurance or trust. At this point in our study of the Psalms, we have therefore arrived at a third major type or theme or voice in the book of Psalms. As we have seen, Psalm 8 is a song of praise, and Psalm 13 is a prayer for help. As a psalm of assurance or trust, Psalm 23 affirms and celebrates the help and provision that God promises. In this sense, it is akin to Psalm 13, especially verses 5–6. But Psalm 23 is also akin to Psalms 1 and 8. By inviting us to receive life as God's gracious gift and to live in humble submission to God and in accordance with God's purposes, Psalm 23 commends a way of living that might be called the lifestyle of praise, or perhaps the "way of the righteous" (Ps. 1:6; see question 2 at the end of chapter 2). The recognition of the kinship between Psalm 23 and Psalms 1, 8, and 13 is further impetus to hear Psalm 23 as a psalm for daily instruction and use, not simply as a psalm for times of distress and extremity.

To begin to put ourselves in touch with the ability of Psalm 23 to shape our daily living, it is important to realize that Psalm 23 does not function in other contexts in the way that it has come to function in the United States—that is, it is not known elsewhere primarily as "a funeral psalm." Jeff Moore, a pastor and teacher who recently returned to the United States after four years of ministry in Lesotho, a small nation in southern Africa, puts it plainly to me in a recent conversation: "Psalm 23 does not mean the same thing in Lesotho as it does in the United States." The main reason for the difference, Jeff explained, is that Lesotho is a rural, agrarian country, and so people in Lesotho are accustomed to seeing shepherds *every day*. Hence, they are much more inclined to hear the shepherd metaphor in Psalm 23 as one that is meaningful for daily life, as well as for situations of death and loss.

A further indication of how Psalm 23 speaks differently in other parts of the world is pointed out by Philip Jenkins:

> Read Psalm 23 as a political tract, a rejection of unjust secu-
> lar authority. For Africans and Asians, the psalm offers a
> stark rebuttal to claims by unjust states that they care lov-
> ingly for their subjects—while they exalt themselves to the
> heavens. Christians reply simply, "The Lord is my shep-
> herd—you aren't!" Adding to the power of the psalm, the
> evils that it condemns are at once political and spiritual,
> forces of tyranny and of the devil. Besides its political role,
> Psalm 23 is much used in services of healing, exorcism and
> deliverance.[3]

Does it ever occur to Christians in the United States to think about Psalm 23 "as a political tract," or as a biblical text that "condemns . . . forces of tyranny"? Probably not, or at least only very rarely. This fact, of course, highlights the value of reading, hearing, and interpreting the Bible in conversation with Christians around the world. As we interpret and appropriate Psalm 23, I suggest that we keep in mind our Asian and African sisters and brothers, from whom we might learn to hear Psalm 23 in a new way. The point is not to diminish the importance of Psalm 23 as a funeral psalm, but rather to extend its ability to speak powerfully beyond situations of extremity and distress. Perhaps we shall even be put in touch with its potential "political role," as Psalm 23 instructs us and equips us to resist tyrannical and demonic forces that are rampant in our world today.

Dimensions of Meaning

Title

Of all the seventy-three psalms associated with David, Psalm 23 is probably the one people most like to think of as having actually been written by David, drawing upon his experience as both a shepherd and musician (see 1 Sam. 16:11–13; 17:34–35; 18:10; 19:9). Even though it is unlikely that David wrote any of the psalms (see the chapter on Ps. 8), it is important not to ignore the mention of David in the title of Psalm 23. To be sure, David was remembered as a shepherd, but more importantly, David was the greatest of the Israelite-Judean kings, so much so that subsequent Judean kings were typically known as "sons of David." Thus, to mention the name of David is to call to mind the whole structure of royalty. In this case, the allusion to royalty may alert the reader not to miss the royal connotation of the term "shepherd" when it occurs in verse 1.

Verse 1

In Israel and Judah as well as generally in the ancient Near East, kings were known as the shepherds of their people. This meant that they were responsible for providing the resources, especially food and protection, that enabled their people to live securely. In the Old Testament, this understanding of kings as shepherds is clearest in Jeremiah 23:1–6 and Ezekiel 34:1–16 (see also Ps. 72), two prophetic texts that criticize the kings-shepherds for not providing for the people. Ezekiel 34:11–16 is particularly reminiscent of Psalm 23 as it portrays God as the good shepherd, who says, in response to the failure of the Judean kings, "I myself will be the shepherd of my sheep, and I will make them lie down" (Ezek. 34:15).

In short, God is the ultimate sovereign, in whom the psalmist rightly places complete trust, secure in the knowledge that "I shall not want," or better translated, "I shall lack nothing." The point is not that the psalmist will get everything he or she asks for or desires, but rather that God will provide all that is *needed* to live securely. In Gerald Wilson's words, "Those who trust in Yahweh as sheep do in a shepherd will never lack for whatever they *need*."[4] A persistent feature of contemporary North American culture is the inability to distinguish between wants and needs, and so Psalm 23 may be able to perform an extremely valuable service for today—that is, it may be able to help us make a distinction between what we want and what we need. In any case, verses 2–3 describe how the shepherd provides what sheep (and people) need to live securely.

Verses 2–3

The pastoral imagery in verses 2–3 has often been understood as communicating primarily a sense of tranquility, rest, and repose. This has been the case especially with the phrases "lie down," "still waters," and "restores my soul." To be sure, this dimension of meaning is not totally absent from verses 2–3—sheep (and people) do need rest and time to recover from the rigors of the day—but the *primary* affirmation of verses 2–3 is that the shepherd provides the sheep with the basic necessities of life. "Green pastures" may be a place where the sheep can "lie down" to rest, but as much or more to the point, "green pastures" means that the sheep will have sufficient food to eat. A location "beside still waters" may be a tranquil place conducive to rest, but as much or more to the point, especially since sheep are afraid to drink from a flowing stream, "still waters" means that the sheep will have easy access to sufficient water to drink. In short, the shepherd provides the two basic necessities that support animal life—food and water. It is the provision of these basic necessities that, from the sheep's perspective, "restores my soul," or better translated, "keeps me alive" (see the NRSV note, which suggests that the Hebrew word often translated "soul" more basically means "life").

A third basic necessity is also in view in verse 3. The shepherd "leads me in right paths," a translation that better fits the metaphor than the more traditional "leads me in paths of righteousness" (KJV, RSV). For sheep, right paths literally mean the difference between life and death. To take the wrong path means to be separated from the shepherd and the flock and thus subject to being lost or attacked by predators (see Ezek. 34:5–6, 12, 16). To be led in "right paths" means safety, security, shelter, protection. The final phrase of verse 3, "for his name's sake," suggests that God provides the fundamental necessities of life—food, water, protection—because it is God's nature or character to do so. The word "name" elsewhere in the Old Testament can connote character. In a word, it is God's character to will and work for *life,* and God is characteristically and consistently committed to providing the fundamental necessities that make life possible. The connection between God's character and God's support for life is evident in verse 6 as well, where a description of God's character ("goodness and mercy") is followed by the affirmation that the psalmist will live securely in God's abiding presence.

Verse 4

The sheep-shepherd metaphor obviously continues into verse 4, but the NRSV rightly sets off verse 4 from verses 1–3, taking a clue from the grammatical shift from referring to God in the third person to speaking directly to God, a more intimate form of address: "for you are with me; your rod and your staff—they comfort me." This poetic line receives further emphasis by the fact that it is exactly the central line of the poem. As is often the case in Hebrew poetry, what is central structurally is also central theologically—in this case, the affirmation of the unfailing presence of God and God's protection for life, even in the midst of the most threatening of circumstances.

Whereas verses 1–3 have in view the shepherd's daily provision of necessities, verse 4 "moves to a description of fearful threat," to use Gerald Wilson's description.[5] Hence, verse 4 is more in keeping with the use of Psalm 23 in crisis situations. The translation "darkest valley" may be more appropriate for the metaphor, as it suggests the rugged, ravinelike streambeds through which shepherd and sheep must sometimes travel in search of food and water. Even so, the underlying Hebrew word does seem to be an unusual compound noun formed from two Hebrew words that mean "shadow" and "death." So the more familiar, traditional translation can be defended, and it has the advantage of articulating more vividly situations of extremity and threat that are traditionally associated with Psalm 23.

The rod and staff are implements carried by shepherds. The staff was used to guide the sheep and perhaps to prod them when necessary. The rod was a shorter stick, probably something more like a club to be used in defending the sheep from predators. The Hebrew word translated "rod" refers in other contexts to a king's scepter, thus recalling the royal connotations of shepherd. God is the ultimate and ultimately reliable sovereign, doing whatever is necessary in ordinary and extraordinary situations to keep the sheep/people alive.

Verses 5–6

Most commentators agree that the metaphor shifts at verse 5 from sheep-shepherd to guest-host. The direct address continues in verse 5 as the guest commends the host for ample provision. In short, what the host does for the guest in verse 5 is what the shepherd does for the sheep in verses 1–4—that is, supplies every need, including food ("a table"), drink ("my cup overflows"), and hospitality/shelter/protection ("you anoint my head with oil"). The correlate of the "darkest valley" (v. 4) seems to be "the presence of my enemies" (v. 5), and again in this section of the psalm, there is nothing to fear. The enemies may be present, but they are clearly not a threat (see the chapter on Ps. 13).

Beyond this conclusion concerning the enemies, it is difficult to assess their significance in the psalm. Some scholars suggest that the original background of verse 5 involved the ancient practice of seeking asylum or sanctuary from enemies in the temple (see Exod. 21:12–14, which reflects such a practice, and in which "my altar" suggests that the temple was a designated place of sanctuary). Other scholars suggest a less specific setting. For instance, the psalmist imagines being hosted by God at a table, while the enemies stand around the walls of the room, to be mocked and taunted by the psalmist as he or she eats. Given the lack of certainty, these proposals may be possible, but it is at least possible to imagine as well that the enemies join the psalmist at the table. In fact, the immediate literary context—that is, the conclusion of Psalm 22— seems to support such an interpretive direction. Like the end of Psalm 23, the conclusion of Psalm 22 describes a meal, probably a communal meal accompanying a thanksgiving sacrifice or "offering of well-being" (see Lev. 7:11–18), portions of which were eaten by the worshiper and others whom he or she invited. But the thanksgiving meal in Psalm 22 is quite unusual. In the psalmist's imagination at least, it is not only "the poor" who "shall eat and be satisfied" (v. 26), but also "all the families of the nations" (v. 27) and even the dead (v. 29) and "future generations" (v. 30). Such an expansive congregation must certainly include the psalmist's enemies! The resulting picture is one in which psalmist and enemies have been reconciled, and it is in keeping with the perspective of the songs of praise, which regularly invite all peoples and nations, and indeed all creation, to worship God (see Pss. 8, 103, 148).

In any case, the enemies are not a threat. This conclusion receives further emphasis in the first poetic line of verse 6, which is better translated, "Surely goodness and mercy [or "steadfast love"] will *pursue* me all the days of my life." The NRSV's "follow" is much too weak, and it misses the allusion to the enemies. Ordinarily in the Psalms, it is the enemies who pursue the psalmist; the underlying Hebrew word is even sometimes translated "persecute." But here, even though the enemies are present, it is God's goodness and steadfast love—two words that serve as an admirable summary of God's character—that pursue the psalmist. In short, to attempt to capture the reversal contained in this wordplay, we might say that it is God's steadfast love which "threatens" or "persecutes" the psalmist—and, of course, this threat is actually a promise! The promise is life, lived securely in the company of God, the gracious host, who supplies every need.

To be sure, the promise of life is a comforting assurance in times of extremity and loss, but it is also meant to be appreciated and appropriated as a daily experience, as is emphasized by the repetition of "days" in the final two poetic lines of the psalm. God's goodness and love pursue the psalmist "all the days of my life," and the psalmist dwells in God's house "for the length of days" (see NRSV note). Everyday, the psalmist finds a home with God. The final stanza of Isaac Watts's metrical paraphrase of Psalm 23 expresses beautifully the daily experience of life in God's household, including God's daily provision of the psalmist's needs:

> The sure provision of my God attend me all my days;
> O may your House be my abode, and all my work be praise.
> There would I find a settled rest, while others go and come.
> No more a stranger or a guest, but like a child at home.[6]

As Watts suggests too, the grateful acceptance of God's gift of life is the foundation of genuine security—"a settled rest" (the Hebrew verb that begins the final poetic line of the psalm could be read as "rest" rather than "dwell")—as well as the starting point for making praise a lifestyle in addition to a liturgical response: "and all my work be praise."

Psalm 23 for Today

We are now in a position, recalling Philip Jenkins, to consider how Psalm 23 can address us today as a "political tract," and to identify some of "the evils that it condemns." An initial clue is the fact that the term "shepherd" was a political title in the ancient Near East. By addressing God as the ultimate shepherd-sovereign, Psalm 23 effectively relativizes all other political claims for our ultimate loyalty and allegiance. Although unlike many of our sisters and brothers in Asia and Africa we do not ordinarily think of our country as an "unjust state," the fact is that the United States, like every other sovereign state, regularly attempts to claim our ultimate loyalty and allegiance. Our leaders frequently attempt to assure us that, regardless of what we may do, God is on our side. Many citizens of the United States, including many Christians, routinely conclude that any criticism of our country and its policies is "unpatriotic." This conclusion affirms, in effect, their opinion that our nation, not God, is ultimately sovereign. At this point, we can learn from our Asian and African friends that Psalm 23 can and should function today as a political tract.

When we consider Psalm 23 and the evils that it condemns, it is again helpful to begin with its affirmation of God as the ultimate shepherd-sovereign. As such, it is God who offers life as a *gift* to us and to all God's sheep/people, along with what is *needed* to sustain life. In short, life and the resources that sustain life are gifts to be *received*, not something simply to be *achieved*. As Henri Nouwen puts it, "All is grace." He continues, "Light and water, shelter and food, work and free time, children, parents and grandparents, birth and death—it is all given to us. Why? So that we can say *gracias*, thanks: thanks to God, thanks to each other, thanks to all and everyone."[7]

The problem with this perspective is that almost no one in North America seems to believe it. In fact, Nouwen says that he literally had to leave the United States in order to learn about grace and gratitude from friends in Latin America. Seldom does it occur to us North Americans that life is a gift, and almost never does it occur to us to be content with what we *need*. Rather, life— or "making a living," as we usually refer to it—is something we work hard to achieve for ourselves, and the measure of our success is our ability to acquire more and more. The result is the virtual inability among us to distinguish between what we want and what we need, and the further result is the creation and perpetuation of a system that rewards excessive individualism and fosters greed. In terms of Psalm 23, Jenkins suggests that "the evils that it condemns" are "forces of tyranny." Our contemporary socioeconomic system is precariously close to being tyrannical, although the danger is so subtle that most of us do not even suspect a thing. Thomas Merton saw the reality clearly:

> Even though there's a certain freedom in our society, it's largely illusory. Again, it's the freedom to choose your product, but not the freedom to do without it. You have to be a consumer and your identity is to a large extent determined by your choices, which are very much determined by advertising. Identity is created by ads.[8]

When identity is created by advertising, the inevitable reality will be greed. In a revealing diagnosis, former Federal Reserve chairman Alan Greenspan suggested several years ago that "our national illness is . . . 'infectious greed.'"[9]

If Greenspan is right—and he certainly spoke authoritatively to the financial community in our country—then it just may be that greed, along with the excessive individualism that drives it, are among the evils that Psalm 23 condemns. But at the same time, Psalm 23 commends the cure to our "infectious greed," as it offers an identity shaped not by ads but by the affirmation that God is our shepherd, that God is the gracious host who freely gives us the gift of life and what is needed to sustain it. If life is a gift, if all is grace, then the appropriate response is gratitude, and gratitude is the cure we so desperately need. Just as we have seen how our Asian and African friends can help us, so, Nouwen suggests, can our Latin American friends:

> A treasure lies hidden in the soul of Latin America, a spiritual treasure to be recognized as a gift for us who live in the illusion of power and self-control. It is the treasure of gratitude that can help us to break through the walls of our individual and collective self-righteousness and can prevent us from destroying ourselves and our planet in the futile attempt to hold onto what we consider our own.[10]

Hearing and heeding Psalm 23 may be able to teach us not only to distinguish between what we want and what we need, but it may also teach us "the treasure of gratitude" that may turn out to be nothing short of life-saving and world-preserving!

One of the fundamentals of Latin American theology is the affirmation that living gratefully—that is, believing in and living by grace—results in pervasive solidarity. The logic is simple: if we believe in and live by grace, then we will not think that we "deserve it" (and that others do not), and we will not posture ourselves as better than other people. Instead, we will be inclined to view others as our sisters and brothers and will be led to share out of an abundance of our possessions and resources.[11] Exemplifying this direction, and thus manifesting an encouraging and curative movement among us, are wealthy entrepreneurs such as Bill and Melinda Gates, Warren Buffet, and Bono. These individuals are exercising creative leadership by giving their money away and by encouraging others to do the same.

In terms of the dynamics of gratitude leading to solidarity, it is important to notice that the psalmist ends up in Psalm 23:6 "in the house of the LORD"—seemingly the temple in the original setting of the psalm but more generally in the presence of God and among God's household or family. As Konrad Schaefer concludes concerning verses 5–6, "The poet voices the community sentiments. The 'table for me' is not a meal in solitude, but a convivial banquet, and the 'house of the LORD' is a public place where the community enjoys worship and public life."[12] Schaefer's comments put us in touch again with the "political role" of Psalm 23. The gracious gifts the psalmist receives are not to be enjoyed in isolation. Rather, they invite and impel the psalmist into the community of God's people. Grace and gratitude inevitably result in solidarity, quite literally, for God's sake (see v. 3).

Christian readers of Psalm 23 will undoubtedly recognize that what the psalm affirms resonates clearly with the gospel of Jesus Christ, who framed his fundamental message in inescapably political terms: "the kingdom of God has come near" (Mark 1:15). One of the primary signs of the kingdom involved how and with whom Jesus ate and drank, and one of the things Jesus explicitly told his followers to do was to continue to eat and drink together in his memory. M. Douglas Meeks suggests that Psalm 23 proclaims the same message contained and enacted in the Lord's Supper:

> The celebration of the Lord's Supper is under orders from God the Economist and is a concrete instance of God's providential *oikonomia* [this Greek word is the basis for the English word "economy," which literally means "law of the household"] with implications for all eating and drinking everywhere. For this reason, the disciples of Jesus should pray boldly for daily bread (Luke 11:13). They should keep the command to eat and drink, recognizing that it includes

the command that they should share daily bread with all of God's people.

... Psalm 23 depicts the work of God's economy overcoming scarcity in God's household.[13]

Because God is the source of all food and drink, and since we belong above all to God's household, we are invited to live under God's sovereign claim and to share our resources with all God's children—the ultimate in solidarity. Psalm 23, as it turns out (like the Lord's Supper), has not only a "political role" but an economic role as well! In our world, in which the paramount moral issue is the continuing existence of life-threatening hunger and poverty in a world of plenty, Psalm 23's invitation for today could hardly be more timely.

While the Lord's Supper casts Jesus in the role of gracious host, recalling Psalm 23:5–6, John 10:1–17 portrays Jesus as "the good shepherd" (John 10:11, 14), recalling Psalm 23:1–4. As in Psalm 23, Jesus leads (John 10:3), feeds (John 10:9), and protects (John 10:12–13), all for the purpose of life (John 10:10). The mysterious reference to "other sheep that do not belong to this fold" (John 10:16) may suggest that God's household is more expansive than we usually think, with room perhaps for "enemies" (Ps. 23:5), and given the similar conclusions to Psalms 22 and 23, maybe even room "for all the families of the nations" (Ps. 22:17).

The inclination toward universality is evident too in the way that the central affirmation of Psalm 23—"you are with me"—relates to the presentation of Jesus, especially in the Gospel of Matthew. Toward the beginning of Matthew, Jesus is to be called "Emmanuel . . . 'God is with us'" (Matt. 1:23), and the conclusion of Matthew returns to this theme, as the risen Christ assures his disciples, "I am with you always, to the end of the age" (Matt. 28:20). This final promise of Emmanuel accompanies the Great Commission to "make disciples of all nations" (Matt. 28:19). God, the ultimate shepherd, sovereign, and host, wills to gather a world-encompassing household—again, the ultimate in solidarity (see Pss. 8, 148). In a world increasingly threatened by economic, ethnic, political, and religious divisions, Psalm 23's invitation to accept life as God's gracious gift, and to share it with the world, is precisely what we need to hear and heed today.

Questions for Reflection and Discussion

1. Related to the traditional interpretation and use of Psalm 23 in the United States, invite members of your group to share experiences involving Psalm 23. In particular, in what situations has Psalm 23 spoken to you and how?

2. The November 2007 issue of *Sojourners* contains an article detailing the activity of Rev. Billy and his "Church of Stop Shopping." It is not really a church but rather a sort of street-theater performance "using the cadences and mannerisms of a TV evangelist" to stage protests against rampant consumerism.[14] Rather than dismissing Rev. Billy as part of the lunatic fringe, *Sojourners* gives him and his "church" serious analytical attention, employing the insights of one of the leading biblical scholars in the world, Walter Brueggemann. Brueggemann concludes that Rev. Billy and his movement are about hope, defined as "the deep conviction that there is a viable, choosable alternative to shopping that will make possible a human community of neighborliness, justice, and peace."[15] What do you think of this definition of hope? How may Psalm 23 contribute toward the realization of such hope?

3. How do you go about distinguishing between want and need? Can Psalm 23 be a help in this process? If so, how? Is greed inevitable in an economic system such as ours?

4. Think further about the Asian and African appropriation of Psalm 23 as a "political tract." Drawing upon the resonances between Psalm 23 and the gospel of Jesus Christ, what would our country look like if we were truly "a Christian nation"? In your view, how can Psalm 23 contribute to the ongoing debate in our nation about authentic patriotism?

5. In commenting on verse 6, Gerald Wilson says, "I dwell in God's house and in his presence whenever I unite with him and his people in service to his world."[16] How does Psalm 23 call us to mission?

Chapter Five

Psalm 32

James Limburg notes that Psalm 32 "has been one of the more popular psalms in the Christian tradition."[1] One indication of its popularity is the fact that it is one of the church's seven penitential psalms (along with Pss. 6, 38, 51, 102, 130, and 143), a grouping that may well have had its origin with Augustine, who reportedly had the text of Psalm 32 posted over his bed so that he would see it every morning before anything else.[2] Even though Psalm 32 contains no actual confession of sin, its report of the psalmist's movement from pained silence (vv. 3–4), to confession (v. 5), to joyful witness to God's faithful, forgiving love (vv. 6–11; see also vv. 1–2) has proven to be extremely influential and extraordinarily powerful. Not surprisingly, the apostle Paul, one of the most influential witnesses to God's grace in the entire history of Christianity, knew Psalm 32 and quoted its opening two verses in Romans 4:6–8, as he made his case for justification by grace—that is, the incredible good news that God sets things right in the world not by punishing but by forgiving! In other words, Paul had learned about grace not only by way of his relationship with the risen Christ but also by reading the Psalms.

Traditional historical-critical Psalms scholarship has had a difficult time categorizing Psalm 32. As Konrad Schaefer observes, "Psalm 32 is a curious combination of thanksgiving and instruction."[3] But this combination is not really so strange.

Having experienced the liberating effects of divine forgiveness, the psalmist not only would have been inclined to give thanks but also would have naturally wanted to share this experience with others. Perhaps as good or better a term than "instruction" to characterize the psalmist's words to others is the term "witness." As Robert Jenson suggests, "The psalmist's own stance is that of *witness*, to his experience and to the grace of God."[4] To be sure, the psalmist addresses God (see vv. 4–7), so at least portions of Psalm 32 may be considered a prayer. But the prayer itself seems intended to be overheard by others, so that Erhard Gerstenberger helpfully concludes that Psalm 32 "comes very close to being a homily on penitence."[5] In short, the inclusion of Psalm 32 among the church's penitential psalms makes good sense. In any case, Psalm 32 has served and continues to serve to put people in touch with the benefits of confession, the liberating effects of forgiveness, and the essentially gracious and loving character of God.

Dimensions of Meaning

Title

As John Goldingay observes concerning the mention of David in the title of Psalm 32, "If one wished to imagine David praying it, then his eventual confession after his affair with Bathsheba and his murder of Uriah would make a telling context."[6] Goldingay is clearly correct, and the Revised Common Lectionary for Year C pairs Psalm 32 with the David-Bathsheba episode, but since the title of Psalm 51 specifically mentions this episode, we shall wait until the treatment of Psalm 51 to explore this context in detail.

The title labels Psalm 32 a *Maskil*, which is a transliteration rather than a translation of the Hebrew. In short, we do not know what *Maskil* means. It is interesting to note that the Hebrew root involved is the same as that of the initial verb in verse 8, "I will instruct." Since Psalm 32 has an instructional orientation, it is tempting to conclude that *Maskil* designates an instructional type of psalm; however, the other psalms bearing this designation in the title do not seem particularly instructional (Pss. 42, 44, 45,

52–55, 74, 78, 88, 89, 142). So the literary link between the title and verse 8 may be coincidental, and certainty is elusive.

Verses 1–2

The most obvious feature of verses 1–2 is the repeated "happy" that begins each verse. As we have seen, "happy" is the very first word in the book of Psalms, so the reader of Psalm 32 is inevitably reminded of Psalm 1. Not coincidentally, it seems, there are several other words and phrases in Psalm 32 that hearken back to Psalm 1: "sin/sinners" (32:1–5), "day and night" (32:4; 1:2), "teach" (32:8; the root is the same as "law" or "instruction" in 1:2), "way" (32:8; 1:1, 6), "wicked" (32:10; 1:1, 4–6), and "righteous" (32:11; 1:6). This shared vocabulary and conceptuality serve to remind the reader to put Psalms 1 and 32 in conversation. When we do so, what we learn is that happiness, which Psalm 1 defines as constant attention to God's law or instruction (Ps. 1:1–2), does not mean perfection or sinlessness. Or to put it even more pointedly perhaps, to be "righteous" does not mean that one has succeeded in doing everything right. Rather, as Psalm 32 makes clear, sin has powerful and pervasive effects in the life of the righteous. To be righteous means, in essence, to be forgiven. Thus, the righteous in the Psalms are those who live by grace.

The other obvious feature of verses 1–2 is the occurrence of several words that communicate disobedience: "transgression" (v. 1), which connotes willful rebellion; "sin" (v. 1), which means essentially to miss the mark, intentionally or unintentionally; and "iniquity" (v. 2), which suggests the destructive and enduring consequences of disobedience and which is often appropriately translated "guilt." These are the three major words in the Hebrew vocabulary of disobedience, and all three will recur in verse 5, each accompanied by the possessive pronoun "my." The effect is to communicate clearly that the life of the righteous is pervaded by sin.

At first glance, the final line of verse 2 may seem to belie this conclusion; it seems to say that the happy ones do not harbor the sin of deceit. But "deceit" here is not really parallel to the three previous words for disobedience. Instead, this final line of verse 2 suggests that happiness derives finally from not having to deny the reality of sin in one's life (see 1 John 1:8). In this respect, the final line of verse 2 anticipates what the psalmist will say in verses 3–5 that he or she finally discovered—namely, that he or she does not have to pretend to be perfect, so the "silence" (v. 3) can be broken and the way be open to receive forgiveness and to reach genuine happiness.

Verses 3–4

Verses 3–4 describe the conditions that prevailed when the psalmist was still practicing "deceit" (v. 2), denying his or her sinfulness, pretending to be perfect. As the psalmist indicates, it was not working. Sin was taking its toll, including severe physical effects. In light of what we know today, we might say that the psalmist was suffering psychosomatic symptoms. Although verse 4 seems to attribute the physical effects to divine judgment—"your hand was heavy upon me"—the reader is left with the overwhelming impression that the real problem is not a vindictive God but rather a deceitful psalmist, that is, that the real problem is the psalmist's "silence" (v. 3). As verses 1–2 make particularly clear, God is more than ready and willing to forgive.

Although in a sense verses 1–5 form a section within the psalm, especially in view of the repetition linking verses 1–2 with verse 5, it is also appropriate to treat verses 3–4 as a separate section, as the NRSV suggests in its layout. The *Selah* following verse 4 reinforces this conclusion. As with *Maskil* in the title, *Selah* is a transliteration rather than a translation. In short, again we do not really know what *Selah* means. It appears to mean something like "lift up," and it perhaps was originally an indication for some sort of liturgical response, perhaps by temple musicians, or a Levitical choir, or even by the gathered worshipers. We simply do not know. In any case, *Selah* often appears at points where a poetic section seems to conclude. This being the case, one might expect a *Selah* after verse 5, and indeed there is one there. The more unexpected *Selah* after verse 4 has the effect perhaps of inviting the reader to linger at least momentarily over the pain and anguish of verses 3–4. The effect too is to set off verse 5, which is both the culmination of verses 1–5 and a turning point in the psalm. Thus, the two occurrences of *Selah*, one right before and one right after verse 5, suggest its pivotal importance.

Verse 5

The three primary words for disobedience recur in verse 5, each accompanied by the possessive pronoun "my." But each of the three words is also the direct object of a verb which makes it clear that the psalmist has broken the "silence" (v. 2)—"I acknowledged," "I did not hide," "I will confess." As John Goldingay observes concerning the psalmist's breaking of the silence, "Keeping quiet is not a mark of OT [Old Testament] piety. OT piety makes a noise. . . . Only noise can bring an end to anguish and wasting, the vocal protest to Yhwh that the psalms keep modeling or the confession voiced in this psalm."[7] The "noise" is immediately effective—"and you forgave the guilt of my sin." The "you," of course, is God, and the appearance of this pronoun is doubly emphatic—first of all because it is not really necessary (the Hebrew verb form itself indicates a second-person singular subject), and secondly because the subject is emphasized by appearing before the verb (thus reversing the normal Hebrew syntax). The emphatic "you" reinforces the conclusion that God is more than ready and willing to forgive. The real problem all along has been the psalmist and his or her "silence."

Adding further emphasis to this final poetic line—and thus focusing the reader's attention on God's willingness to forgive— is the fact that it is nearly, or perhaps precisely (depending on how one arranges and counts the poetic lines), the central line of the psalm. As we saw in Psalm 23, what is central structurally is often of central importance theologically. Here it is forgiveness. Then too, "forgave" in verse 5 repeats the same Hebrew verb that underlies "forgiven" in verse 1, and the repetition emphasizes even further the importance of forgiveness. This verb means "forgive" only in a figurative or extended sense. The fundamental sense of the verb is "to lift, bear, carry." Thus, the implication is that God is willing to "carry" our sin; we might also say that God is willing to bear the burden of sin and guilt that rightfully belongs to us. Of course, this is grace in its purest form. As James Mays rightly recognizes, the psalmist's "silence" had been "the rejection of grace."[8] No wonder the apostle Paul quotes Psalm 32:1–2 in Romans 4:6–8!

There is one more instance of repetition linking verses 1 and 5 and highlighting the importance of the psalmist's breaking of the "silence" in order to open himself or herself to God's grace. The Hebrew word translated "covered" in verse 1 occurs again in verse 5, where it is translated "hide." When the psalmist stops *covering* his or her sin, as in "cover up," then God *covers* the sin, as in the phrase "I've got it covered." Again, God is ready and willing to forgive; grace is quintessentially important. The psalmist, who clearly has sinned, will later include himself or herself among "the righteous" (v. 10). Again, the significance of this fact can hardly be overemphasized, in terms of understanding the Psalms or understanding biblical faith more generally—that is, righteousness derives not from doing everything right but from confronting and confessing one's essential sinfulness and living in fundamental dependence upon the grace of God.

Verses 6–11

Those who have genuinely experienced forgiveness will want to share the good news of God's grace. So it is with the psalmist. That verse 5 is a turning point in the psalm is evidenced by the fact that the vocabulary of disobedience—sin, transgression, iniquity/guilt—does not occur again. From verse 6 onward, the psalmist is a joyful and enthusiastic witness to God's transforming work. Immediately after the affirmation "you forgave," the psalmist addresses others, inviting their response in prayer. What was said above of "the righteous" applies also to "all the faithful"—that is, the "faithful" are not those who have done everything right but rather those who break the silence of self-reliance to accept the grace of God. The Hebrew root underlying "faithful" is the same one represented by "steadfast love" (v. 10). "Steadfast love" lies at the heart of God's character (see Exod. 34:6–7, where God's "steadfast love" is manifest by God's willingness to forgive, and see the commentary on v. 6 in the chapter on Ps. 23). Thus, it might be more accurate and helpful to translate verse 6a as follows: "Therefore let all who are steadfastly loved offer prayer to you." What was said above about praise applies also to prayer— that is, prayer becomes more than a liturgical action. It is also the lifestyle of those who renounce self-reliance in order to accept and live by the grace of God.

In verse 7, the psalmist returns to his or her own prayer, with three affirmations about God to match the three I-statements in verse 5. The "you" that begins verse 7 is the same pronoun that began the final line of verse 5; the focus is again clearly and emphatically upon God, to whom the psalmist witnesses. The vocabulary of verse 7 anticipates verses 10–11. The word "surround" occurs in verses 7 and 10, and "glad cries" in verse 7 is the same Hebrew root that recurs in verse 11 in verbal form as "shout for joy." The repetition emphasizes the transition that has taken place. "Silence" and "groaning all day long" have been replaced with a pervasive sense of God's all-encompassing love, and the formerly withering and withdrawn psalmist (vv. 3–4) is now virtually jumping for joy and inviting others to join the celebration. The two additional verbs in verse 11—"be glad" and "rejoice"— reinforce the changed mood and the dramatic rise in energy level. The literary links among verses 6–7 and 10–11 also call attention to what may be an intentional *abcb'a'* (chiastic) structural pattern:

a	invitation to others (v. 6)
b	affirmation of faith (v. 7)
c	instruction (vv. 8–9)
b'	affirmation of faith (v. 10)
a'	invitation to others (v. 11)

As the outline suggests, the effect of such a pattern is to highlight the middle element, the instruction in verses 8–9. Even so, it is not entirely clear who is speaking in verses 8–9. Is the "I" the psalmist who continues to speak as a witness, or is the "I" to be understood as God, who speaks a word perhaps delivered originally by a priestly spokesperson in the context of worship? A case can be made for either option, but in the final analysis, it probably does not matter. For what is clear is that "the way you should go"—and the "you" includes us contemporary readers of Psalm 32—is the way the psalmist has described and exemplified. It is the way that rejects the stubborn (v. 9), strength-sapping "silence" (v. 3) of self-reliance in favor of the honest, humble confession of sin and need that means the acceptance of grace, along with the promise of joy (vv. 7, 11) and genuine happiness (vv. 1–2).

If the psalmist is speaking in verses 8–9 (see the chapter on Psalm 51, in which the forgiven sinner becomes a teacher of others), the point is not boasting about his or her own "getting it together." Rather, the witness is to God (v. 7) and to God's unfailing "steadfast love," or as James Limburg translates *hesed*, God's "amazing grace."[9]

It may not be coincidental that Psalm 33, which uncharacteristically contains no title, echoes the invitation issued by the psalmist in 32:11. This suggests, in essence, that Psalm 33 constitutes the content of the "shout for joy" mentioned in 32:11. That content is joyful praise, appropriately involving "a new song" sung by those who have been made new by God's amazing, transforming grace. And appropriately too, the "new song" celebrates God's "steadfast love" (vv. 5, 18, 22), which, the psalmist now affirms, not only "surrounds those who trust in the LORD" (32:10) but also fills "the earth" (33:5).

Psalm 32 for Today

In his comment on Psalm 32, Erhard Gerstenberger points out that "facing up to one's errors and being pardoned are important modes of interaction even today, which go far beyond all the existing penitential rites of religious and ideological groups."[10] He is certainly correct, and his observation may explain why confession seems to be so popular in some circles today. Many people seem willing to go on television, for instance, and confess all sorts of wrongdoings. What they usually do *not* do, however, is repent, and almost never is the word "sin" used. Even among us Christians, who do have various traditions and rites of confession, there is often a reluctance to see ourselves as sinners. In a recent sermon, after noting the popularity of confession in the media and popular culture, Diane Santelli concluded, "It seems like the church is the only place confession is on the decline."[11] She may be right, and the reason probably has to do with the problematic word "sin."

Noted psychiatrist Karl Menninger observed several years ago that the word "sin" had virtually disappeared from our vocabulary. In his book *Whatever Became of Sin?*, Menninger proposed that we recover the word and the concept:

> My proposal is for the revival or reassertion of personal responsibility in all human acts, good and bad. Not total responsibility, but not zero either. I believe that all the evil-doing in which we become involved to any degree tends to evoke guilt feelings and depression. These may or may not be clearly perceived, but they affect us. They may be reacted to and covered up in all kinds of escapism, rationalization, and reaction or symptom formation. To revive the half-submerged idea of personal responsibility and to seek appropriate measures for reparation might turn the tide of our aggressions and of the moral struggle in which most of the world population is engaged.[12]

Menninger articulates what Psalm 32:3–4 also suggests—that is, sin creates feelings of guilt that, if not acknowledged and confessed, "affect us" in debilitating ways. Like the psalmist, Menninger suggests that we break the silence; or, as he puts it, we need "to study sin"—not to get better at it, of course, but rather "to spur measures for combating and rectifying it."[13]

One of the dimensions that needs to be considered as we "study sin" involves an exploration of the reasons for our reluctance to acknowledge and confess our sins. In reflecting upon the contemporary significance of Psalm 32, Gerald Wilson suggests two such reasons. The first is what Wilson describes as "the fierce independent streak that characterizes much of our society."[14] This is akin to what I labeled as *autonomy* in the chapter on Psalm 1, and it leads, in Wilson's opinion, to an excessive "concern for personal privacy"[15] that means we are hesitant to reveal our innermost selves to others, especially aspects of ourselves that may make us look bad. This leads to Wilson's second reason, which he describes as "a sense of perfectionism that pervades much of Western Protestantism."[16] Even when we know we are not perfect, we think we *should* be; consequently, we often feel compelled to *pretend* that we are. Such pretending, however, is difficult to maintain indefinitely, and as Menninger suggests, the unconfessed and unresolved guilt works itself out in other ways— depression, escapism, rationalization, and reaction or symptom formation.

As evidence for this dynamic, Wilson points to the large number of people in 12-step groups, "people who followed their sense of powerlessness [what Menninger calls "depression"] and fear of being discovered as they really were into years of hiding their fears in a variety of destructive behaviors: alcoholism, drug addiction, sexual compulsion, eating disorders, gambling addiction, and many, many others." As Wilson also points out, the fifth step of Alcoholics Anonymous is this: "Admitted to God, to ourselves, and to another human being the exact nature of our wrongs."[17] He concludes that this is genuine confession; indeed, it has proven for many persons to be a major step toward transformation and wholeness.

It is no wonder that writer and theologian Frederick Buechner suggests "that the church has an enormous amount to learn from" 12-step groups:

> These groups have no buildings or official leadership or money. They have no rummage sales, no altar guilds, no every-member canvass. They have no preachers, no choirs, no liturgy, no real estate. They have no creeds. They have no program. They make you wonder if the best thing that could happen to many a church might not be to have its building

burn down and to lose all its money. Then all that the people would have left would be God and each other.[18]

These words from Buechner are found in a memoir entitled *Telling Secrets*, and in essence this is what Psalm 32 is about—breaking the silence, sharing those secrets we are all too inclined to hide, hurting ourselves and others in the process.

The point in acknowledging and confessing our sinfulness is not to make ourselves feel guilty. As both Menninger and Wilson suggest, we *already* feel guilty, consciously or unconsciously. The point is to prevent guilt from taking its destructive toll—in short, the point is forgiveness or grace. One scholar who has recently been studying sin in detail is Mark Biddle, and he makes this point well: "The gospel message is less about the fact that human beings *cannot* earn worth in God's eyes because they are inherently unworthy and more about the fact that human beings *need not* earn God's regard because God has already given it as a gift."[19]

Psalm 32 is clearly about sin, but it is just as clearly about the forgiveness of sin and the joyful, liberating, healing effects of being forgiven. It is no coincidence that the apostle Paul heard in Psalm 32 the gospel message, the good news that God sets things right by being gracious rather than punitive. The tragic thing about the church's reluctance to talk about sin is this: If we do not talk about sin, then neither will we talk genuinely about grace. And if we do not talk genuinely about grace, then we simply will not understand the gospel. In the final analysis, then, Psalm 32 is a vitally important resource as we "study sin" and as we study grace.

Questions for Reflection and Discussion

1. Discuss John Goldingay's conclusion that Old Testament piety "makes a noise." How might you or we be more "noisy" in the expression of our faith or piety?

2. Although the ancient psalmists would have had no concept of psychosomatic symptoms, can Psalm 32 illumine our understanding of such phenomena? Is it possible that

being more honest with ourselves and with God might make us feel better and more vital?

3. How does our culture encourage and reinforce the privatism and perfectionism that, as Wilson suggests, contribute to our hesitancy to confess our sinfulness? Can Menninger's suggestion that we "study sin" help us to avoid the pitfalls?

4. Confession of sin in the Reformed tradition tends to take place in corporate prayers of confession during Sunday morning worship services, as opposed to the Roman tradition of confessing sins to a priest. What might be the advantages and/or disadvantages of each tradition? Are there other practices, liturgical or otherwise, that might enable us more adequately to confess our sins?

5. What are some ways that Christians together can more effectively serve as witnesses to God's "amazing grace"?

Chapter 6

Psalm 51

What James Limburg says about verses 2–5 of Psalm 51 actually applies to the entire psalm—that is, it provides "a short course on the Old Testament notions of sin and forgiveness."[1] In this respect and several others, Psalm 51 has much in common with Psalm 32. Like Psalm 32, Psalm 51 is one of the church's seven penitential psalms, and very appropriately, it is the psalm assigned for Ash Wednesday in all three yearly cycles of the Revised Common Lectionary.

In contrast to Psalm 32, which reports on the liberating effects of confession and forgiveness, Psalm 51 contains an actual confession of sin (vv. 3–5), along with a series of requests for forgiveness, reconciliation, and renewal (vv. 2, 6–12, 14–15). Like Psalm 32 again, however, Psalm 51 ultimately has an instructional orientation (vv. 13, 16–19), and in the final analysis, again like Psalm 32, the instruction is about grace. In this regard, it is revealing that before the vocabulary of sin is introduced, verse 1 is dominated by the vocabulary of divine grace: "mercy," "steadfast love," and "abundant mercy" (a different Hebrew root from the first instance of "mercy" in this verse). Thus, Psalm 51 offers us further opportunity to reflect upon God's amazing grace and its meaning for today. The radical character of divine grace is particularly evident when we read Psalm 51 in the context of the story of David, Bathsheba, and Nathan, as the title invites us to do.

Dimensions of Meaning

Title

Psalm 51 is one of thirteen psalms that cite in the title a specific episode in the life of David (see also Pss. 3, 7, 18, 34, 52, 54, 56, 57, 59, 60, 63, and 142). Such Davidic titles were probably added to these psalms by editors of the book of Psalms at a relatively late period in the history of the book's collection and transmission. Although these titles may not be historically accurate, they should by no means be ignored. The editors of the book of Psalms recognized that certain psalms would have been appropriate for David to have prayed at crucial points in his life, and thus they invite readers of the book of Psalms in every generation to hear certain psalms in a particular narrative context.

In the case of Psalm 51, the narrative context is the familiar story that begins with David's adulterous relationship with Bathsheba (see 2 Sam. 11:1–12:15). David is eventually confronted by the prophet Nathan, at which point he recognizes and confesses his sin with these words: "I have sinned against the LORD" (2 Sam. 12:13). Nathan announces to David that "the LORD has put away your sin" (2 Sam. 12:14), although there will be consequences for David's disobedience. Thus, there is a good fit between David's experience and Psalm 51, so much so, in fact, that at least one contemporary historical critic concludes that David really did pray Psalm 51.[2] Who knows? In any case, if David did not pray Psalm 51, he certainly *should* have prayed it (or something like it)!

To hear Psalm 51 as David's prayer and testimony is to appreciate the radicality of divine grace. After all, David had violated at least half of the Ten Commandments—he coveted Bathsheba, his neighbor's wife; he stole her from her husband, Uriah; he committed adultery with her; he lied about it; and when the lies did not work, he had Uriah killed. And yet, despite the extent of his disobedience, and despite the fact that he had committed capital offenses, David was forgiven! So, whether David actually prayed Psalm 51 or not, we should have him and his experiences in mind as we interpret Psalm 51 and consider its implications for today.

Verses 1–6

The vocabulary of divine grace dominates verse 1 and precedes the first mention of sinfulness ("transgression," in v. 1b). This vocabulary of grace suggests that we hear Psalm 51 not only in the context of the narrative of David and Bathsheba, but also in the context of another narrative of blatant sinfulness—namely, the golden calf episode in Exodus 32–34. In Exodus 32, shortly after having promised to obey God in every way (see Exod. 24:3, 7), the people of Israel violate the first two commandments: they worship another god by making a graven image (see Exod. 20:3–6). God is outraged and is initially inclined to punish, but after Moses' intercession for the people, the narrative recounts that God "changed his mind about the disaster that he planned to bring on the people" (Exod. 32:14). The only explanation for such a change of mind is offered by God's self-revelation to Moses in Exodus 34:6–7. Three of the key words that describe God's character in Exodus 34:6—"merciful," "gracious," and "steadfast love"—are also found in Psalm 51:1 (even though the NRSV uses "mercy" to render the two different Hebrew roots represented by "merciful" and "gracious"). In short, the psalmist appeals to the character of God that had been manifest at a crucial point in the people's history, when they, like David, had sinned grievously.

The final line of verse 1 introduces a series of three requests for forgiveness that continues through verse 2. Each verb is followed by one of the basic words in Israel's vocabulary of sin—"transgressions," "iniquity," and "sin" (see the commentary on vv. 1–5 in the chapter on Ps. 32). Each of these three words is repeated at least one more time in verses 1–5 (NRSV's "iniquity" in v. 2 and "guilty" in v. 5 translate the same Hebrew word), and a fourth item is added in v. 4—"evil." The effect is to indicate emphatically that the psalmist's life is pervaded by sin. The content of the confession reinforces this perception. The psalmist is constantly aware of being sinful (v. 3) and affirms unambiguously that God is "justified in your sentence" (v. 4). The first line of verse 4 does not seem to apply too well to David, whose sin clearly affected other people, not just God. But the intent of verse 4a may be to suggest that every action which harms other people results fundamentally from a failure to obey God. As Konrad Schaefer concludes concerning verse 4a, "A crime against the neighbor is an offense against God."[3]

Verse 5 has been a focal point in the church's formulation of a doctrine of "original sin." This is appropriate, as long as we realize that the psalmist had no intention of formulating this or any other doctrine. As Schaefer puts it, verse 5 is "sheer exaggeration"—that is, poetic hyperbole that intends to communicate "the deep-rooted predicament of the self."[4] In short, verse 5 is clearly *not* meant to convey that sin is something like a sexually transmitted disease. Rather, the "predicament of the self" to which it points is the reality that sin pervades the human situation and that none of us can finally, despite our best intentions, escape sin and its effects.

Even so, verse 6 eloquently affirms that sin is not ultimately determinative in the human situation. God desires "faithfulness" (NRSV, "truth"), and the psalmist requests that "God cause me to know wisdom" (NRSV, "teach me wisdom"). The repetition of the verb "know" recalls verse 3, where the psalmist "know[s]" his "transgressions." But here, a different knowledge is possible. Sin is not the final word. Rather the final word is the "wisdom" that derives from attentiveness to God's ways and from living in fundamental dependence upon God rather than self. Verse 6 serves a transitional function, recalling the confession of sin that begins verse 3 and simultaneously initiating another round of petition that continues through verse 12 and that will eventually portray more fully the new, transformed self the psalmist becomes.

Verses 7–12

The same three verbs that occurred in the requests of verses 1b–2 occur again in verses 7–9 but in reverse order (the NRSV translates

the same Hebrew verb as "cleanse" in v. 2 and "purge" in v. 7), perhaps signaling the reversal the psalmist experiences. Reinforcing
this reversal is the fact that the vocabulary of sin, which was represented twelve times in verses 1–9, is represented only twice in
verses 10–19. Simultaneously, whereas God was mentioned
explicitly only once in verses 1–9, God is mentioned six times in
verses 10–19. As Schaefer observes:

> Sin, remarkably present in the beginning, gradually disap-
> pears and is replaced by God in the latter part. To be more
> precise, sin disappears in the second half in the same ratio
> that God appears; thus, with the confession sin is replaced by
> God's presence. The poet literally and literarily is emptied of
> sin and filled with grace.[5]

The experience of God's gracious presence means the possibility
of joy, as suggested by the three different Hebrew words for joy
in verse 8, anticipating verse 12 as well as the singing and praise
of verses 14–15.

The reversal—that is, the transformation of the psalmist into a
renewed, joyful self—is perhaps most clear in verses 10–12. The
initial request, "Create in me a clean heart," employs a verb that
is used in the Old Testament only of God's creative activity. It is
especially frequent in the opening chapter of Genesis, which also
features "spirit" (Gen. 1:2), a word occurring three times in suc-
cessive verses (Ps. 51:10–12). The effect, especially in view of the
word "new" in verse 10b, is to suggest that God's gracious presence has transformed the psalmist into nothing short of "a new
creation" (see 2 Cor. 5:17–20, where "a new creation" results from
God's "not counting their trespasses against them"; see also Rom.
12:1–2).

The mention of God's "holy spirit" in verse 11 is unusual and
occurs elsewhere in the Old Testament only in Isaiah 63:10–11. It
may serve here to communicate the radicality of grace, since ordinarily, holiness means standing apart from any source of taint or
pollution. For God to reach out to the profoundly and pervasively
sinful psalmist in order to create a "clean heart" (v. 10), and then

to remain with the psalmist (v. 11), suggests that God's will to forgive motivates God to compromise or redefine God's holiness (see Hos. 11:9, where God is "the Holy One in your midst"—that is, in the midst of a blatantly sinful and rebellious people, whom God ultimately refuses to reject or stand apart from). In a sense, grace means that God does new things! And God's renewing work means renewal for the psalmist.

The phrase "joy of your salvation" (v. 12a) is better understood when we realize that in the Old Testament, "salvation" is the restoration of conditions that make possible the life God intends. In Psalm 51, the life God intends is thwarted by the psalmist's own sinful self-assertion. Hence, "the joy of your salvation" means something like the experience of joy that results from receiving life as a gift of God's grace. The mention of "salvation" in verse 12a anticipates verse 14, where "O God of my salvation" could be translated, "O God who gives me life." The appropriate response to grace seems to be in view in verse 12b, where "a willing spirit" probably refers to generosity. Having received a gift, the appropriate response is to give in return, to share. Those who know that life is a gift will inevitably be both grateful and generous. The psalmist's gratitude and generosity will be evident in the subsequent verses.

Verses 13–17

The psalmist's generosity—that is, giving back to God and to others—is evident in verse 13. The same Hebrew verb underlies "restore" in verse 12 and "return" in verse 13, and the repetition both reinforces the reversal that has taken place and communicates the psalmist's generosity. That is, having been the beneficiary of God's restorative work (v. 12), the psalmist now is involved in the restoration of others, by way of a teaching ministry (v. 13). It may seem strange, even somewhat arrogant on the psalmist's part, now to be teaching "transgressors" and reaching "sinners," since the psalmist had been immersed in "transgressions" (vv. 1, 3) and sin (vv. 2, 3, 4, 5, 9). But what the psalmist is witnessing to is not his own achievement of "getting his life together," but rather to the transforming, renewing power of God's grace.

The request in verse 14, "Deliver me from bloodshed," may be another prayer for forgiveness, if "bloodshed" means the guilt that was incurred from being a violent person (as David was). On the other hand, the psalmist's request may be for protection from violence, now that he has become a witness to God's grace. One thinks, for instance, of a later witness to God's grace—namely, the apostle Paul. Having been transformed by grace from a murderer (as David had been) to an evangelist, Paul incurred the wrath and violence of those who were offended by his proclamation of "justification by grace"—that is, his claim that God sets things right not by punishing but by forgiving. In this regard, it is worth noting that the word the NRSV translates as "deliverance" in verse 14 is more literally "righteousness" or "justification." The same Hebrew word appeared in verse 4 as "justified," and a reversal is again evident. The psalmist's justifiable sentence has been commuted. Although guilty, he has been pardoned. Things have been set right, or justification has occurred, through grace. It is about such amazing grace that the psalmist teaches.

Such testimony is a concrete manifestation of the gratitude expressed as well by the psalmist's singing (v. 14) and declaration of praise (v. 15). Every organ of speech is involved—"tongue," "lips," and "mouth"—emphasizing the psalmist's depth of gratitude. If, as I have suggested, a genuine experience of grace issues in gratitude and generosity, it also inevitably yields humility, as verses 16–17 bear witness. Recalling Psalm 50:23 and its definition of acceptable sacrifice as "thanksgiving" or gratitude, verse 17 complements Psalm 50:23 by adding that God wants people to offer "a broken and contrite heart." The word "broken," which also modifies "spirit," should be heard not in the sense of dysfunctional, but in the sense of humble. The mention of "spirit" and "heart" recall verses 10–12, leading to the conclusion that the truly "clean heart" is the humble heart. The rhetorical effect of verses 13–17 is finally to communicate the crucial lesson that gratitude, generosity, and humility go hand in hand as a response to divine grace.

Verses 18–19

Commentators often conclude that verses 18–19 are a later addition to an earlier version of Psalm 51 that ended at verse 17, and this may be correct. It does seem that someone wanted readers of Psalm 51 not to conclude that corporate worship—which in ancient times integrally involved "sacrifices" and "burnt offerings" (v. 19)—was unnecessary or unimportant. As in Psalm 50:23 and 51:16–17, the prophets frequently offered criticisms of sacrifice (see Isa. 1:10–20; 58:1–14; Hos. 6:6; Amos 5:21–24; Mic. 6:6–8); these criticisms, however, were not meant to denigrate worship in general but rather worship that was empty of ethical content, or worship that aimed at providing religious sanction for self-aggrandizement. Indeed, by and large, the Psalms were derived from and were used in the liturgical life of ancient Israel and Judah. In short, the Psalms portray worship as an important, indeed essential, component of a proper relationship with God. But, like anything else, worship can be infected by sin. Psalm 51 suggests that worship is genuine and faithful when it involves gratitude to God, humility before God, and generosity to others in God's name.

In any case, the effect of verses 18–19 is to provide a corporate conclusion to a prayer that had been voiced exclusively in the first person in verses 1–17. We are thus reminded that sin and its effects are not simply personal and private, but rather that sin and its effects should also be analyzed in corporate, institutional terms. In fact, it is particularly important to consider structural sin as we address the significance of Psalm 51 for today.

Psalm 51 for Today

Given the similarities between Psalms 32 and 51, it is not surprising that an engagement with Psalm 51 should help us to continue what we began in conversation with Psalm 32—that is, to "study sin." In this case, the concluding two verses of Psalm 51 prove to be very valuable, warning us not to reduce sin to merely a personal, private matter. Douglas John Hall describes well the state of the study of sin in recent years:

> Ever since Karl Barth, Paul Tillich, and Reinhold Niebuhr . . . theology has been attempting to recover something of the more penetrating meaning of the elusive term sin. It is perhaps the most misunderstood word in the Christian vocabulary. Most people in the churches seem still, despite half a century of serious and critical reflection on the subject, to think of sin in rather crudely moralistic terms—in terms, to be explicit, of private morality, with special emphasis on private sexual morality. No one is surprised . . . when . . . adultery [is] described as sinful. But how many of our fellow citizens would think of connecting sin with the arms race, or the greed of the First World, or ecological disasters created by high technology? Even the association of sin with humanity's reputedly "greatest" achievements and successes, and with what individuals are prone to consider their best and most honorable deeds—even such an association, though it is as old as the prophets of Israel, seems difficult for our contemporaries to grasp.[6]

The relatively recent history of the United States seems to bear out the accuracy of Hall's observations. In the late 1990s, when it was revealed that President Bill Clinton had been unfaithful to his wife, the national news was full of talk about sin. One major network even featured on its evening news a major story about sin, repentance, and forgiveness, complete with a chart outlining the Christian, Jewish, and Muslim views on these subjects. But a few years earlier, when President Ronald Reagan and then Vice President George Bush lied to the people of the United States for years about covert arms sales to Iran that were illegally financing the Contra War against the Nicaraguan government, there was no public discussion about sin and repentance, even when the scandal broke and even though 30,000 people died as a result of the war.

In the wake of the Enron and WorldCom scandals and other corporate misdeeds, there was talk of unethical behavior and criminal activity, but the word "sin" seldom, if ever, entered the public discussion. And today, when ecological catastrophe seems more imminent than ever, there is little inclination to diagnose the problem in terms of human sin. In these crucial matters of our public life, it might help us to turn things around—which is what repentance literally means—if we would identify what is going on as sin.

To be sure, not all voices are silent in this regard. Jim Wallis and his Sojourners organization issued the following call to repentance, coinciding with the fifth anniversary of the Iraq War: "As U.S. Christians, we issue a call to the American church to lament and repent of the sin of this war."[7] Regardless of whether one agrees with Wallis and the statement, we should notice carefully that Wallis and Sojourners are true to the spirit of Psalm 51—that is, they are taking the lead in challenging us to reintroduce the vocabulary of sin and repentance into the public discussion of a crucial contemporary issue. The same can be said of the recent attempt by the Vatican to broaden the notion of sin to include social as well as individual sins. As Vatican spokesperson Gianfranco Girotti put it recently, "Attention to sin is a more urgent task today precisely because its consequences are more abundant and more destructive."[8]

While Psalm 51 encourages and assists us to continue to study sin, it also (and again like Ps. 32) encourages and assists us to continue to study grace. In this regard, Gerald Wilson refers to "the value of sin" and describes it as follows: "The one true value invested in our forgiven sin is this possibility of testifying to the gracious mercy of God."[9] When Psalm 51 is heard as David's testimony, the witness to God's grace is all the more remarkable. As we have seen, the story of David, Bathsheba, and Nathan in 2 Samuel 11–12 reveals David to be not only a covetous adulterer but also a thief, a liar, and a murderer. To be sure, David's despicable behavior had disastrous consequences in the life of his family, but David is forgiven, and he is not even removed from office. The cynical observer may interpret all this as just one more instance of a rich and powerful person being above the law and quite literally getting away with murder. But the tradition has appropriated David's experience as a witness to God's amazing grace. Not coincidentally, the apostle Paul knew Psalm 51 (see

Rom. 3:4), and he echoes the testimony to God's amazing grace in passages such as Romans 12:1–2 and 2 Corinthians 5:17–20. Remember that Paul himself was a murderer. Indeed, Paul's primary message is that God has acquitted or "justified by his grace" (Rom. 3:23) a pervasively sinful humankind that deserved condemnation (see Ps. 51:4). In short, this is for Paul the message of the cross. And it is amazing that God's strategy to set things right in the world—that is, God's pursuit of justice—is forgiveness rather than punishment.

The radicality of the message of the cross, which is in direct continuity with the message of Psalm 51, is expressed strikingly by William Placher: "It is not just that we should stop scapegoating the innocent, but that we should stop punishing the guilty." Acknowledging the practical challenges of such a strategy, Placher nonetheless concludes:

> There are legitimate concerns about protecting the innocent and rehabilitating those who have gone down wrong paths, but for Christians the condemnation of sinners is no longer possible without condemning Christ. We should not settle for a theology that gives us less than that, for without that we have good news only for those who count themselves among the righteous, and good news only for the righteous is not the gospel.[10]

In the final analysis, it is truly remarkable that the compilers of the books of Samuel chose to include in 2 Samuel 11–12 such an embarrassing story about King David, Israel's greatest king, who was remembered in the tradition as the founder and patron of Israel's worship. And it is equally remarkable that the compilers of the Psalms chose to link Psalm 51 explicitly with David's embarrassing behavior. The lesson is simple but profound—that is, David and Psalm 51 should serve as models for us to accept embarrassment as a clue to repent and as a first step in being transformed. In the late seventh century BCE, the prophet Jeremiah diagnosed the predicament of Judah's national life in terms of the inability to be embarrassed: "They did not know how to blush"

(Jer. 8:12). In our day, Walter Brueggemann has adopted this verse as the foundation for the goal of contemporary Christian education. As he puts it, "I've been thinking that church education ought to be teaching people how to blush."[11] Perhaps the most significant service that Psalm 51 can offer for today is to teach us how to blush!

Questions for Reflection and Discussion

1. Theologian Shirley Guthrie maintains that the work of God's Spirit "can be summarized with the word *new*" (see Ps. 51:10–12).[12] But many people seem to believe that nothing really new is possible in the world. What do you think? Can God's grace make us new? The church new? The world new? Discuss Psalm 51:10–12 in conversation with 2 Corinthians 5:17–20.

2. Although the hymn "Amazing Grace" is immensely popular, it seems that grace may be *too* amazing for us to live by, especially if it means that, in Placher's words, "we should stop punishing the guilty." How might we at least begin to live nonretributive, grace-filled lives?

3. David was a murderer, as was the apostle Paul. How might Psalm 51 and its message of grace help us to think about the issue of capital punishment?

4. How would our Christian education programs be different if their purpose was primarily (or maybe even tangentially) to be teaching people how to blush? What should we be blushing about as individuals, as churches, as a nation, and as a world?

5. Henri Nouwen said he had to leave the United States in order to learn about grace and gratitude. How does American culture discourage the formation of persons in the direction of gratitude, generosity, and humility?

Chapter Seven

Psalm 63

L ove Song" is the title Konrad Schaefer gives to Psalm 63, and indeed the psalm is a powerful expression of the tie that binds someone's life to God in love (see especially v. 3).[1] Because the opening verb of the psalm, which the NRSV translates as "seek," can also mean "to look for dawn," Psalm 63 has traditionally been used by the church as a morning psalm. But beyond this use, Psalm 63 has enjoyed wide popularity. Several major figures in the history of Christianity considered Psalm 63 their favorite psalm, including John Chrysostom, Thomas à Kempis, and Protestant reformer Theodore Beza, who regularly recited Psalm 63 as part of his evening routine.[2] The key word in Psalm 63 is "soul" (vv. 1, 5, 8, and again in v. 9 where the NRSV translates the Hebrew as "life"), which more accurately means something like "self" or "whole being" or "life." For today, Psalm 63 invites us to consider what truly constitutes *life* for us in our time and place.

Dimensions of Meaning

Title

As with Psalm 51, the editors of the book of Psalms invite the reader to hear Psalm 63 in the context of the life of David; however, the information here is much less specific than in the title of Psalm

51. The editors seem to have in mind the material in 1 Samuel 21–31, in which David is in the wilderness. At two points (1 Sam. 23:14–15; 24:2), Saul seeks to kill David, and the editors of the Psalter may have associated Psalm 63:9 with this aspect of David's experience in the wilderness.

Verses 1–4

In verse 1, the psalmist expresses the need or longing for God in terms of desperate thirst. Water, of course, is a basic necessity of human life, and as verse 1 suggests, the lack of water can lead to weakness. The mention of "soul" and "flesh" should not be understood as indicating a dualism of spirit versus body. Actually, because the Hebrew word translated "soul" means the whole self or being, including the flesh or body, in essence the psalmist is saying that his or her whole being desperately longs for God as a fundamental necessity of human existence. Relationship with God is not simply one option among others; rather, it is absolutely necessary for life.

Therefore, it is logical that the psalmist looks for God in God's place—"the sanctuary"—where God's "power and glory" can be seen (v. 2; see Ps. 27:4). Psalm 29 invites "heavenly beings" to recognize God's "glory and strength" (v. 1; the same two Hebrew roots as in Ps. 63:2), and Psalm 29 concludes with an affirmation of God's sovereign claim on the whole cosmos (v. 10). In Psalm 63, the psalmist is certainly aware of having been claimed by God, and thus of belonging intimately to God. The appropriate response is the entrusting of the self fully to God in a sort of sweet surrender. This faith posture is described beautifully and memorably in verse 3: "Because your steadfast love is better than life, my lips will praise you." James L. Mays characterizes as follows the experience the psalmist so poetically describes: "Trust becomes for a moment pure adoration that leaves the self behind as any participant in the reason for adoration. . . . This verse leads us in prayer to the point of devotion to God alone that must be the goal of all true faith."[3] In other words, verse 3 represents a sort of self-denial that paradoxically means the discovery of the fullness of life as God's gracious gift. Thus, the psalmist anticipates Jesus' teaching that those "who want to save their life will lose it, and those who lose their life for my sake, and for the sake of the gospel, will save it" (Mark 8:35).

As verses 3–4 suggest, the lifestyle of those who are devoted "to God alone" will consist of "praise," submission (the word "bless" seems to have meant originally to kneel in subservience or submission), and prayer. The ancient posture of prayer involved uplifted hands rather than bowed heads (see Pss. 28:2; 134:2), and prayer embodies essentially a yielding of the self to God's "steadfast love" and an entrusting of the self to God's provision, which will be celebrated in verse 5.

Verses 5–8

This central section of the psalm is bounded by references to "my soul" in verses 5 and 8, signaling that the real subject of the psalm continues to be *life*. Here again, as in verses 1–4, the psalmist affirms that he or she is intimately related to God and provided for by God. Whereas it is thirst that God quenches in verses 1–4, it is hunger that God addresses in verse 5, and the psalmist is abundantly "satisfied" (see also Pss. 65:4; 81:16; 107:9; 132:15). As in verse 3, so in verse 5 the psalmist's response to God's gracious, abundant provision is praise. The psalmist's "lips" are again involved, and this time "my mouth" as well. Verse 6 may suggest prayer, recalling verse 4; but in any case, it indicates the psalmist's complete devotion to God, as God occupies his or her thoughts not just every waking moment but also every sleeping moment. This complete orientation to God recalls Psalm 1:2, which commends meditation on God's instruction "day and night." In both cases, the constant meditation upon God and/or God's purposes is a source of "joy" (Ps. 63:7) or "delight" (Ps. 1:2).

The depth of the psalmist's trust in God is expressed again in verse 7: "For you have been my help." At least implicitly, the psalmist renounces self-help, choosing to live instead in fundamental dependence upon God and God's provision for life (see the chapter on Psalm 23; see also "help'" in Pss. 22:19; 27:9; 40:17). The phrase "in the shadow of your wings" may allude to the winged creatures that attended the ark in the temple (see Pss. 17:8; 36:7; 57:1). If so, perhaps this is further indiction that the psalmist is "in the sanctuary" (v. 2). In fact, especially on the basis of verses 2, 6, and 7, some scholars hypothesize that Psalm 63 may have originated while the psalmist conducted a vigil, spending the night in the temple to celebrate intimacy with God and the reality of having been helped and provided for by God. To be sure, it is not necessary to take the imagery of verses 2, 6, and 7 literally. It is entirely possible to construe it metaphorically. For instance, "the shadow of your wings" may constitute a metaphor for God as a mother bird, gathering and protecting her young beneath her wings. In any case, it is clear that the language and imagery of Psalm 63 have functioned metaphorically for generations of the faithful, who have used the words of the psalm to express their own trust in God's life-giving, nurturing, protecting presence.

Verse 8 continues to communicate the intimate connection between self and God that sustains the psalmist's life. The verb "clings" is used in Genesis 2:24 to express the bond between husband and wife, who have left mother and father and "become one flesh." And it is used elsewhere in the Old Testament, especially in the book of Deuteronomy, to communicate the covenant relatedness of the people and God (see Deut. 10:20; 11:22; 30:20; NRSV, "hold fast" or "holding fast"). In both Deuteronomy 11:22 and 30:20, the verb occurs in sequence with "loving the LORD." The intimate connectedness with God that the psalmist articulates and celebrates in Psalm 63 does indeed make it, as Schaefer suggests, a love song.

The imagery of being provided drink (vv. 1–4) and food (vv. 5–8) by the God who claims us and to whom we are intimately connected will remind Christian readers of the Lord's Supper. Like the psalmist, we Christians in the sacrament renounce self-help and self-provision, professing instead that our lives and everything that sustains us are ultimately God's gracious gift. Quite appropriately, and again quite in keeping with the tone of Psalm 63, the Lord's Supper is known as "the joyful feast of the people of God."[4]

Verses 9–11

The profound depth of the psalmist's joy is evident in verses 9–11, where we learn that the psalmist's rejoicing takes place amid threats to his or her life. As we have seen, verse 9 may have motivated the editors of the Psalter to link Psalm 63 with David, whose life was threatened by Saul. Beyond this linkage, however, the threatened psalmist belongs in a much larger company of those whose lives were threatened: other psalmists (see Pss. 35:4; 38:12; 54:3), Moses (Exod. 4:19), Elijah (1 Kgs. 19:10, 14), Jeremiah (Jer. 11:21; 26:8), and Jesus (Mark 3:6; 11:18). In each of these cases, the threatened ones entrusted life and future to God and thus were emboldened and empowered to persevere in the face of opposition.

Such trust includes even the ability to rejoice amid suffering (see Heb. 12:2), and as verse 9 suggests, it also includes the ability to believe that God and God's purposes will ultimately prevail. This is the function of the language and imagery that describe the demise of the psalmist's opponents—their descent into "the depths of the earth" (v. 9; see Ps. 86:13), their being "given over to the power of the sword" (v. 10), their becoming "prey for jackals" (v. 10), and their "mouths" being "stopped" (v. 11). While it is important to recognize that the psalmists regularly express their trust in the ultimate enactment of God's purposes, it is also important to recognize that the enemies are virtually omnipresent in the Psalms. Apparently, God does not simply obliterate the enemies in some sort of swift, unilateral action. Rather, trusting God and the ultimate fulfillment of God's purposes, the psalmists experience the life-giving, life-sustaining presence and power of God amid ongoing threat—that is, their faith enables them to rejoice in the midst of suffering. Or to again use James L. Mays's phrase (see the chapter on Ps. 13), for the psalmists "the agony and the ecstasy belong together."

Even so, it is interesting to note what we might call the "poetic justice" expressed in verses 10–11. Whereas the psalmist eats and "is satisfied with a rich feast" (v. 5), the opponents will be eaten—"they shall be prey for jackals" (v. 10). Those who seek to perpetuate violence as they "seek to destroy" the "life" of the psalmist (v. 9) will themselves become the victims of violence—"they shall be given over to the power of the sword" (v. 10). In essence, the psalmist comprehends and expresses the futility of violence—"those who live by the sword will die by the sword." Although here and elsewhere the psalmists envision a justice that may not get worked out immediately and to their personal benefit, they never abandon the hope that God will ultimately set things right, and thus they are energized to persevere, to live faithfully and joyfully in the face of persistent, powerful, and even life-threatening opposition.

The significance of the mention of "the king" in verse 11 is not clear. Some scholars suggest that the king—David or otherwise—should be understood as the one who prayed this psalm originally (as the editors of the Psalter seem to want to communicate), but if so, it is not clear why the king would now switch to the third person in verse 11 to refer to himself. It is just as likely, or more likely, that the psalmist concludes his or her prayer by mentioning the king in conjunction with the vision of the ultimate accomplishment of God's will. It was the king, after all, who was responsible for the earthly enactment of God's will, including the responsibility to "crush the oppressor" (Ps. 72:4), a specific instance of which is described in Psalm 63:9–11. In any case, it is clear that the reference to the king in verse 11 did not prevent later generations of the faithful from claiming Psalm 63 as their own articulation of profound connectedness to and hope-filled trust in God.

The final affirmation of the psalm—"the mouth of liars will be stopped"—reinforces again the psalmist's faith in the eventual enactment of God's purposes. The final verb, "stopped," is connected by Hebrew alliteration to the opening verb, "seek," and the wordplay also serves to reinforce the psalmist's trust in the life-giving purposes of God. While "the mouths of liars will be stopped," the "mouth" of those who "seek" God will be open as it joyfully "praises" God (vv. 1, 5). In the final analysis, both poetically and theologically, the "stopped," closed mouth symbolizes death, resulting from violent opposition to God and God's purposes, whereas the open, praise-filled mouth symbolizes life as God intends it. As Claus Westermann suggests, in terms of the Psalms, to praise God is to live.[5] The psalmist in Psalm 63 is a stellar example, for here, the psalmist prays to live (vv. 4, 6) and lives to praise (vv. 3, 5, 11; the NRSV's "praises" in v. 5 and "exult" in v. 11 translate the same Hebrew root, while "praise" in v. 3 translates a different but synonymous root).

Psalm 63 for Today

One afternoon in January 2001, I sat with a group from Eden Theological Seminary in a room at the central offices of the Roman Catholic Archdiocese of Guatemala, just off Guatemala City's central plaza and a short way down the street from Guatemala's National Cathedral. We were being addressed by José Antonio Puac, who throughout the 1990s had served as an assistant to Bishop Juan Gerardi, who had headed a very important project for the archdiocese's Office of Human Rights. The goal of the project was to document as fully as possible the stories of the people who had disappeared or been killed in Guatemala's prolonged civil conflict in the years between 1961 and 1996, the year in which the peace accords were signed. The effort was known as the Recovery of Historical Memory Project, and much like South Africa's Truth and Reconciliation Commission, it aimed to tell the violent truth about the past several years, not as a basis for prosecuting the perpetrators of violence but rather as a foundation for a new way forward for the people and nation of Guatemala.[6] The Recovery of Historical Memory Project Report was presented publicly by Bishop Gerardi from the steps of the National Cathedral on April 24, 1998. Two days later, it became starkly apparent that certain parties in Guatemala did not want the truth to be known and told when Bishop Gerardi was brutally murdered as he returned to the rectory that was his home.

José Antonio told us that since that tragic day in 1998, he has dedicated his life to continuing what his mentor and friend, Bishop Gerardi, had begun—that is, telling the truth, which in this case means continuing to publicize as widely as possible the results of the Recovery of Historical Memory Project. He realized, he told us, that his own life was thereby endangered. This fact became uncomfortably evident to us when, at one point in his presentation, José Antonio got up and closed the door to the room in which we were meeting. "There is a military office across the courtyard," he explained, "and I don't want anyone over there to hear what I am telling you." When we asked José Antonio why and how he continued his work, in the face of opposition and even threat to his life, he said something like this: "I know this is what

God wants me to do, and God will give me the courage and the strength to go on." He then reminded us that Jesus never promised his followers that it would be easy to follow him.

Such courage and faith to persevere in the face of deadly opposition is what Julia Esquivel, in a wonderful turn of phrase, calls being "threatened with resurrection." Esquivel is a Guatemalan citizen whose life was threatened in the civil conflict and who had to leave Guatemala to live in exile for seventeen years. In her poem "They Have Threatened Us with Resurrection," she honors the many Guatemalans who dared to resist the right-wing death squads and who lost their lives in the process. They were, she affirms, "threatened with resurrection."[7]

The intimate connection to God that enabled the psalmist in Psalm 63 to praise God and "sing for joy" (v. 7) in the face of deadly opposition (v. 9) certainly anticipates what Esquivel calls being "threatened with resurrection." She, of course, is simply being faithful to the Pauline tradition. Paul claimed the power of resurrection as the incredible force that enabled him and others of the earliest Christians to put themselves "in danger every hour" and to "die every day" (1 Cor. 15:30–31).

It is with good reason, especially in view of verses 3 and 9, that Psalm 63 has been associated in the history of its interpretation "with martyrs who valued God more than life and gave up their lives rather than deny their testimony."[8] Although there are martyrs in our time, such as Juan Gerardi and Oscar Romero and Martin Luther King Jr., those who chose to remain faithful even unto death, we North American Christians will not likely face such deadly opposition on account of our faith.

But, as Gerald Wilson suggests, Psalm 63 should serve as an invitation to us to consider the depth of our commitment to God and God's purposes for the world:

> What would we be willing to die for today? Not too much in our comfortable society. Perhaps we would give up our lives for family—that is, our spouses or children. But our psalm tells us that God's love . . . is "better than life itself." . . . Is there some way here and now that the love of God . . . makes that kind of difference in your life? Does it make such a difference

that it wouldn't be worth living without? Is your connection with God so important to you that you would sacrifice all your future hopes and dreams to keep connected to God?[9]

If it seems too threatening for us to consider what we would be willing to die for, then we might ask instead what we are willing to live for. Psalm 63, after all, is about life and about what truly constitutes life, as the repeated word "soul/life" suggests (vv. 1, 5, 8, 9). To use the language of Psalm 63, we might ask what truly *satisfies* us (v. 5), or what makes us sing for joy (v. 8). For many people in "our comfortable society," as Wilson puts it, the goal of life seems to be making a living—that is, working hard in order to make more money for ourselves and our families, so that we can buy more of the things by which we define success or "the good life." The frequent irony of living to succeed by worldly standards is that we are left empty and dissatisfied. Jesus once said that "life does not consist in the abundance of possessions" (Luke 12:15), but in our comfortable society, consider how difficult this is to believe!

Given the pervasive dissatisfaction in our comfortable society, and given the alarmingly high rates of suicide in our culture, it is all the more important that we ask ourselves what we are willing to live for. A recent article in the *Cleveland Plain Dealer* reported on a study that had discovered a 20 percent increase in the number of suicides between 1999 and 2004 among people aged 45 to 54. As one crisis counselor summarized the situation, "A recurring theme in suicide notes is a former breadwinner who can't support family and feels worthless."[10] In short, there are apparently all too many people who live simply to make a living. At the point of economic downturn or setback, they are left with no spiritual resources—no reason to live. It is a contemporary tragedy, suggesting the life-and-death importance of Psalm 63 and its invitation to live first and foremost for God and God's purposes in the world.

In addressing North American Christians for whom actual poverty is ordinarily not a personal problem, Latin American theologians Leonardo and Clovis Boff commend what they call "evangelical poverty"—that is, a manner of living in which people voluntarily seek to live more simply, for God's sake, and in solidarity with the economically poor of our world. In "our comfortable society," we probably will not evoke deadly opposition if we attempt to pursue a lifestyle of "evangelical poverty," but almost certainly we will stand out as noticeably different from our culture." To be sure, being different in this regard does not equate to martyrdom; but it is nonetheless a price we might pay for our willingness to attempt to profess with our lips and portray with our lives that God's "steadfast love is better than life." And in the process, we may discover, paradoxically, that in a way our comfortable society cannot even begin to imagine, we will be singing for joy!

Questions for Reflection and Discussion

1. Psalm 63 articulates clearly the psalmist's urgent longing for God. Consider what it is that we tend to long for urgently or desire fervently. How are our longings and desires shaped by "our comfortable society"?

2. Years ago in examinations of candidates for ordained ministry in the Reformed churches, it was not unusual for someone to ask a candidate, "Would you be willing to be damned for the glory of God?" This question seemed to be designed to elicit the kind of conviction expressed by the psalmist in verse 3. Today the question sounds silly to us—but is there anything to it?

3. Consider further Julia Esquivel's notion of being "threatened by resurrection." What might complete devotion to God and trust in God's future "threaten" us to do in "our comfortable society"?

4. Might there be some connection between what we would be willing to *die* for and what we are willing to *live* for? If so, how?

5. Is it proper to suggest that an embrace of "evangelical poverty" may be a very modest form of martyrdom in "our comfortable society"? In any case, how will devotion to God alone set us over against the values and priorities of our culture?

Chapter Eight

Psalm 73

Psalm 73 is a highpoint in the Psalter," according to John Goldingay.[1] And the exalted opinion of Psalm 73 is even more pronounced in the work of F.-L. Hossfeld and Erich Zenger, who conclude that Psalm 73 "is one of the 'peak texts' of the First Testament."[2] Perhaps the primary reason that Psalm 73 is such an important text, both within the book of Psalms and the entire Old Testament, is that it considers and addresses a fundamental theological question that has occurred to people in all times and places—as Hossfeld and Zenger put it, "the question about the 'place' and 'kind' of God's presence in this world."[3] In this regard, Psalm 73 has much in common with the book of Job, another classic text in the Old Testament.

The book of Job is often labeled a "theodicy," a word composed of two Greek words that together mean "the justice of God." More specifically, where is God's justice in a world where the righteous suffer and the wicked prosper? Or, as Rabbi Harold Kushner suggests in his popular treatment of the book of Job, another way to pose the issue is this—when bad things happen to good people.[4] This framing of the question can be related especially to Psalm 73:13–14, where the psalmist complains of being "plagued" and "punished," despite being innocent. Of course, the question can be posed in the reverse manner—namely, when good things happen to bad people—and such a manner is actually more prominent in Psalm 73. This experience of reality is where the psalmist begins the description of his or her crisis of faith (see vv. 2–3, which are followed by an extended description of "the prosperity of the wicked" in vv. 4–12), which culminates in verses 13–14.

But, of course, Psalm 73 does not end with the crisis of faith. Rather, there is a turning point that begins in verse 13, where the psalmist reaches his or her low point; is focused in verse 15, where the psalmist comes to his or her senses; and continues through verse 17, in which the realization of verse 15 is apparently confirmed in some sort of worship experience. In any case, after verse 17, everything is different. Whereas the psalmist was on slippery ground in verses 1–3, he or she perceives in verses 18–20 that the wicked are actually the ones about to slip. Whereas verses 4–12 contain an extended description of the prosperity of the wicked, verses 21–28 contain a substantial description of the prosperity of the psalmist. To be sure, this newly discovered prosperity is of a different nature than that described in verses 4–12. It does not consist of physical appearance or material things but rather involves the realization of a profound and unbreakable connection with God, even, indeed especially, in the midst of suffering (vv. 23–28)

The structure of Psalm 73 can be outlined in three major sections, each of which begins with the same Hebrew particle (translated "truly" in vv. 1, 18 and "all" in v. 13), as follows:

Section 1   vv. 1–12 The Crisis of Faith (12 lines)
                      vv. 1–3 The plight of the psalmist (3 lines)
                      vv. 4–12 The prosperity of the wicked
                      (9 lines)
Section 2   vv. 13–17 The Turning Point
Section 3   vv. 18–28 The Resolution (12 lines)
                      vv. 18–20 The plight of the wicked (3 lines)
                      vv. 21–28 The prosperity of the psalmist (9 lines)

As the outline demonstrates, there is a certain balance or symmetry between sections 1 and 3, the effect of which is to emphasize the psalmist's transformed understanding of both God and of what constitutes true goodness or prosperity.

The genre of Psalm 73 is difficult to identify with precision. At certain points, the psalmist addresses God directly, so the psalm is a prayer (vv. 13–15, 18, 21–25, 27), with elements of both complaint (vv. 13–14) and a combination of thanksgiving and trust (vv. 23–25, 27). At other points, God is spoken about (vv. 1, 17, 26, 28). This, plus the fact that even those portions of the psalm that address God directly seem to be designed to be overheard by others, makes Psalm 73 into something like an affirmation of faith. In this direction, Erhard Gerstenberger suggests that Psalm 73 has the character both of a "Sapiential, exemplary MEDITATION" and "a dramatic CONFESSION of faith,"[5] and Konrad Schaefer concludes that Psalm 73 is "a community instruction."[6] In short, we stand to learn something very important from Psalm 73.

The significance of Psalm 73 as a "highpoint" or "peak text" may be reinforced by its placement within the book of Psalms. It is the opening psalm of Book III (Ps. 73–89); and probably not coincidentally, it recalls Psalm 1, in which the wicked are also prominent characters (see also "perish" in Pss. 1:6 and 73:27), and also Psalm 2 (see "refuge" in Pss. 2:12 and 73:28). In a real sense, Psalm 73 rehearses the message a reader of the Psalter would have learned by first reading Psalms 1–2 and then continuing through Psalms 3–72—that is, true happiness or goodness does not derive from physical or material prosperity but rather involves the experience of God's enduring presence in all circumstances, including life's worst. For this reason, Walter Brueggemann concludes, "I suggest that in the canonical structuring of the Psalter, Psalm 73 stands at its center in a crucial role. Even if the Psalm is not literarily in the center, I propose that it is central theologically as well as canonically."[7] In short, the central, pivotal placement of Psalm 73 matches its crucially important content, to which we now turn in more detail.

Dimensions of Meaning

Title

Psalm 73 is designated "A Psalm of Asaph," initiating a collection of such psalms (Pss. 73–83) that begins Book III (see also Ps. 50). Asaph is mentioned in 1 Chronicles 6:39; 9:15; 16:5, 7, 37; 25:1–3, 6, in the Chronicler's accounts of preparations for worshiping God. In 1 Chronicles 16:4–5, Asaph is named "the chief" among the Levites who served "as ministers before the ark of the LORD, to invoke, to thank, and to praise the LORD, the God of Israel." Thus, Asaph seems to be the ancestor of a Levitical guild that had certain responsibilities for worship. The Asaphites may well have been responsible for writing some psalms, as well as collecting and editing them, and perhaps leading the performance of them in worship services. Another Levitical guild, the Korahites, is associated with Psalms 42–49, a collection that initiates Book II (Pss. 42–72), as well as with Psalms 84, 85, 87, and 88.

Verses 1–12

Psalm 73 begins with a profession of faith, which should be translated in accordance with the Hebrew text: "Truly God is good to Israel, to those who are pure in heart" (v. 1; see NRSV note, and see also Ps. 24:4). There is no need to emend the text to read "upright," especially since the worshiping community of God's people—"the circle of your children"—will play a key role at the turning point of the psalm (v. 15). While the psalmist rehearses this appropriate confession of faith to begin the psalm, it becomes immediately clear that he or she is having difficulty believing it. The crisis of faith is articulated in verses 2–3 and is precipitated by "the prosperity [Hebrew *shalom*, often translated "peace"] of the wicked."

In short, the psalmist is tempted to conclude that his or her faith is not "working"; it is not paying off in the kind of physical benefits and material rewards that are being enjoyed by the wicked. The wicked's "prosperity" is described in some detail in verses 4–12. They live a wealthy, carefree existence (vv. 4a, 5, 12), they look good (vv. 4b, 7a), and they are respected, influential, and powerful (see v. 6a, which Goldingay translates, "thus prestige has bedecked them").[8] Verse 10 is unclear, but it seems to suggest that the wicked attract a following—that is, some of God's people have not managed to resist the temptation the psalmist was experiencing. As is often the case with rich and influential people, the wicked can get away with a lot—"violence" (v. 6b), deceit (v. 8a), "oppression" (v. 8b). They oppose God, and they dismiss the possibility that God or anyone else might hold them accountable (vv. 9, 11). And they seem to be right! Thus, the psalmist is "envious" (v. 3) and tempted to abandon the faith that seems to be getting him or her nowhere.

Verses 13–17

Verses 13–14 could be considered the culmination of verses 4–12, as the division of material in the NRSV suggests. But the Hebrew particle that begins verse 13 (NRSV, "all") also begins verses 1 and 18, and it seems to be a structural marker, setting off verses 13–17 as a central section between the symmetrical sections formed by verses 1–12 and verses 18–28 (see the outline above). In any case, the psalmist hits bottom in verses 13–14, apparently concluding that faithfulness to God and worshiping God are "vain" or pointless. He or she seems ready to abandon the faith statement with which Psalm 73 begins (note the repetition of "heart" linking vv. 1 and 13). Whereas the wicked are "not plagued" (v. 5), the psalmist is "plagued" continuously (v. 14). So what good does it do to be faithful?

But as close as he or she comes to abandoning faithfulness, the psalmist resists the temptation to join the wicked, as verse 15 indicates. Verse 15 is precisely the middle verse of the psalm, as if to suggest that the psalmist's faithfulness hinges on the recognition that he or she is a part of the larger community—"the circle of your [God's] children." And this recognition is crucial; it is the turning point that keeps the psalmist faithful. James Limburg summarizes the importance of verse 15 as follows:

Psalm 73 also points to the importance of the present community of believers. As long as this person kept these doubts
[vv. 13–14] to himself, he was more and more wearied with
trying to understand the prosperity of the wicked. Then, as
he joined the community of worshipers, somehow he saw
how these people's lives would end up. He would never have
made it alone with his doubts. The community of believers,
which brought him into the presence of God, helped him
find a way through.[9]

In other words, the psalmist would never have arrived at some resolution to the crisis of faith without the support of others.

The further account of some resolution to the crisis comes in
verse 17. It is not exactly clear what is meant by the "sanctuary of
God." The phrase is actually plural in the Hebrew, "sanctuaries of
God," but the plural seems to refer to the various courts or loca-
tions within the temple complex. In short, it is where God's people gather in the presence of God that the psalmist receives some
sort of revelation concerning the wicked and their seeming prosperity. Here the psalmist "perceives their end." It is a new understanding that anticipates the transformation which will be
described in verses 18–28.

Verses 18–28

Given the pervasive presence of the wicked in the book of Psalms
(and in the world, then and now), it is not likely that the psalmist
came to understand that God literally destroys the wicked,
although verses 18–19 seem to suggest such a conclusion. Rather,
more like verse 20 seems to communicate, the psalmist probably
came to understand that the prosperity of the wicked described in
verses 4–12 is illusory—that is, it is not true *shalom*, not genuine
and enduring peace and well-being.

Verses 21–22 look back upon the temptation the psalmist has
managed to resist (see especially vv. 3, 13–14). The prepositional
phrase that concludes verse 22 is more literally "with you." It has
a negative connotation in verse 22—"like a brute with you"—but

it anticipates the two more positive occurrences of the phrase in verses 23 and 25 (NRSV, "but you"). The repetition and wordplay emphasize what the psalmist now realizes is genuine prosperity—that is, being with God, no matter what. Physical and material circumstances have not necessarily improved (see v. 26), but the psalmist needs nothing other than God's presence, of which he or she is now assured (vv. 25–26).

The depth of trust in and desire for God alone that is expressed in verses 23–26 is primarily what causes commentators to view Psalm 73 as a "highpoint" and "peak text." Schaefer adds that "verse 25 approaches a spiritual summit in the First Testament,"[10] and Brueggemann asserts that verses 23–26 "are among the most powerful, daring, and treasured in the Psalter."[11] Some commentators have even heard in verse 24b an articulation of resurrection, the "afterward" being understood as "after death." While this is possible—there are hints of something like resurrection elsewhere in the Psalms (see Pss. 22:29; 49:15)—it is not likely that verse 24b is meant to communicate a doctrine of resurrection. Rather, it is another expression of the intimate connection between the psalmist and God—that is, another way the psalmist claims that I am "with you." Given the fact that the Hebrew word translated "honor" connotes in some contexts material wealth, verse 24b may also suggest that in contrast to the material wealth of the wicked (v. 12), the psalmist receives from God an even greater wealth—the genuine richness of the continual divine presence.

In a real sense, the psalmist has discovered or rediscovered what Psalm 1 defines as true happiness—that is, intimate and unbroken connection with God (see the chapter on Ps. 1). Thus, it is not surprising that the conclusion of Psalm 73 in verses 27–28 recalls Psalms 1 and 2, by way of the words "perish" (v. 27; see Pss. 1:6; 2:12) and "refuge" (v. 28), which is explicitly linked to happiness in Psalm 2:12. The phrase "but for me" at the beginning of verse 28 recalls the identical (in Hebrew) "but as for me" in verse 2, thus contrasting the psalmist's crisis of faith with the newly found assurance. The word "good" in verse 28 also recalls the beginning of the psalm (see v. 1). Now the psalmist knows truly and personally what it means that "God is good to Israel"—that is, God's presence is enduring and unfailing, so that God is always there as a reliable "refuge," no matter what (see v. 26). The psalmist's transformation is marked also by the word "tell" (v. 28), which represents the same Hebrew word that is translated "talk" in the pivotal verse 15. The psalmist has moved from talking about how pointless faith seems to be (vv. 13–14) to talking about "all your [God's] works." Once in danger of joining the wicked in their self-assertion over against God (see especially v. 11), the psalmist is now an eloquent witness to God and the enduring benefits of being "near God" (v. 28). Nearness to God, the psalmist now affirms, constitutes true wealth and the essence of goodness.

Psalm 73 for Today

One of the primary features of contemporary religious life both in the United States and beyond is the prevalence of what is generally known as "the prosperity gospel." According to proponents of this perspective, God want you to be materially rich—and you can be, if you trust God enough and if you follow a set of prescribed steps, ordinarily ones laid out by a self-appointed "evangelist" or "prophet." The promises of the prosperity gospel are illusions. By and large, the only ones who get rich are the evangelists or prophets, whose set of prescribed steps stipulate that their followers should send money to them. Nonetheless, because it promises a quick fix, and because it plays right into the contemporary propensity to define life in terms of material abundance, the prosperity gospel maintains a wide appeal.

In a real sense, the psalmist in Psalm 73 is tempted by something like an ancient version of the prosperity gospel. To be sure, the wicked in the psalm renounce God (vv. 9, 11), and thus they are not manipulating religion in the way that contemporary proclaimers of the prosperity gospel are doing. Even so, what tempts the psalmist is the apparent reality that, like the wicked (vv. 10–12), he or she could be rich and able to live the easy life. In other words, the psalmist nearly concludes that faith is worthless or pointless because it does not seem to work—that is, it does yield the physical benefits and material rewards the wicked are enjoying.

Aside from explicit followers of the prosperity gospel, there seem to be many people who tend to think, at least implicitly, that faith should somehow "work" or "pay off" for them. They are inclined to view faith as something like an insurance policy against sickness, setback, and suffering. But this is clearly not the biblical understanding of faith or faithfulness. The unanimous witness of the psalmists, the prophets, and Jesus himself is that faithfulness to God evokes hostility and opposition—that is, the faithful can expect to suffer. As Jesus issued the invitation to discipleship, "If any want to become my followers, let them deny themselves and take up their cross and follow me" (Mark 8:34; see the chapter on Pss. 13 and 63).

As opposed to the prosperity gospel, the gospel of Psalm 73— which is congruent with the good news contained in the prophetic canon, the book of Job, and the New Testament—is that God is a never-failing presence and source of strength for those who trust God and entrust themselves to God. In a sense, we might say that Psalm 73 affirms that faithfulness is its own reward—not a reward that is guaranteed by good behavior but rather a reward that consists of the continual experience of God's presence and power. The good news of Psalm 73 thus anticipates the apostle Paul's conviction that "neither death, nor life, nor angels, nor rulers, nor things present, nor things to come, nor powers, nor height, nor depth, nor anything else in all creation will be able to separate us from the love of God in Christ Jesus our Lord" (Rom. 8:38–39). As the preceding verses in Romans 8 indicate, it was this profound trust that strengthened Paul to endure hardship, distress, persecution, famine, nakedness, peril, and sword. In short, to claim the faith and to borrow the words of the psalmist, the promise is that we are continually with God (see Ps. 73:25) no matter what. A life lived in such profound trust is the most rewarding life possible, far more rewarding than the physical pleasures and material benefits the wicked enjoy. This is what the psalmist learns in his or her crisis of faith, and this is what the psalmist is determined to "tell" (v. 28) others, including us.

Strengthened by the never-failing presence of God, we are fortified not only to resist the appeal of blatant forms of the prosperity gospel, but we are also equipped to resist the more subtle temptations of our culture to define ourselves by what we have, or how we look, or how much influence we can wield, rather than by our membership in "the circle of your [God's] children" (v. 15). Over against virtually every cultural or worldly standard, we know as God's children that genuine goodness and enduring happiness derive from being "near God" (v. 27) and from representing God's purposes in the world—that is, telling of all God's works (v. 28).

In reflecting upon what faith and faithfulness would look like today in our North American cultural context, William Placher writes the following:

> The only way to communicate Christian faith with passion in a culture like ours without asserting cultural dominance in a way that is offensive to our neighbors and at odds with the central themes of the Christian stories is to keep rejecting the advantages that Christianity's residual cultural status could provide. We Christians have to keep making ourselves into outsiders who can speak with a prophetic voice.[12]

Although Placher refers to "the central themes of the Christian stories," these themes have been anticipated in the Old Testament, including Psalm 73. In effect, the psalmist chooses to make himself or herself into an outsider, to stand over against the apparent prosperity of the wicked, even when others are choosing to join them (v. 10). In our place and time, even if there may be some rewards or advantages deriving from "Christianity's residual cultural status," the faith and the witness of the psalmist can move us to reject them, for God's sake. Our reward, our advantage, will be different. Our purity of heart and purpose will be "rewarded," in essence, by the assurance of being with God. At this point, the good news of Psalm 73 anticipates the Beatitudes: "Blessed are the pure in heart, for they will see God" (Matt. 5:8).

Questions for Reflection and Discussion

1. Why do bad things happen to good people (and vice versa)? How might Psalm 73 help to give us a more in-depth perspective?

2. People often say that they do not need to go to church to worship God, but for the psalmist, participation in the community of God's people was crucial and transforming. Is it possible to be faithful in isolation? What does one stand to miss by not participating in a community of faith?

3. Are there aspects of North American culture that reinforce the appeal of "the prosperity gospel"? If so, what are they and how do they do so?

4. In Placher's terms, are there certain rewards or advantages that derive from "Christianity's residual cultural status"? If so, do you agree that we should reject them? Does Psalm 73 provide encouragement or guidance in this direction?

5. Think about your own life and faith. What does it mean to be "near God"? How might you join the psalmist in the commitment to tell of all God's works?

Chapter 9

Psalm 90

L ike Psalm 73, Psalm 90 occupies a crucial place in the book of Psalms. It begins Book IV (Pss. 90–106), following Psalm 89, which concludes Book III with a poignant lament over the demise of the Davidic monarchy (Ps. 89:38–51). Recent Psalms scholarship has concluded that Books I–III of the Psalter took shape prior to Books IV–V. And since Book III (Pss. 73–89) contains several communal laments that seem to reflect the destruction of Jerusalem (see Pss. 74, 79, 80, 83) and that lead up to the culminating lament in Psalm 89, it appears that the final form of Books I–III has been shaped in response to the defeat of Jerusalem in 587 BCE, the overthrow of the Davidic monarchy, and the subsequent Babylonian exile.

If this is the case, it may explain why Book IV begins with the only psalm in the Psalter attributed to Moses, and why it features an important collection of psalms (Pss. 93, 95–99) that proclaim God reigns. Moses presided over the people before they possessed a land, a temple, a monarchy—all the things that were lost in 587 BCE—and Moses led the people when they understood that their king was God (see Exod. 15:18, where the celebration of the exodus from Egypt culminates in the profession "The LORD will reign forever and ever"). In short, Psalm 90 and Book IV as a whole seem to be designed in part as a response to the crisis of exile and its aftermath, by offering a Mosaic perspective on reality—that is, that a relationship with God is still possible even without land, temple, and monarchy.

Such a reading of Psalm 90 complements the traditional reading of the psalm as a meditation on human transience (see especially vv. 3–10). To be sure, Psalm 90 can profitably be read as such a meditation, but construing Psalm 90 as a response to the exile from a Mosaic perspective provides an additional dimension to this interpretive direction. The exile and its aftermath were vivid reminders of human transience and the impermanence of human structures and institutions (see Isa. 40:6–8 and Ps. 103:15–16, which are similar to Ps. 90:5–6). Furthermore, the character Moses is a striking study in the brevity of human life. Despite his heroic status as liberator, leader, and lawgiver, Moses died before entering the promised land. In essence, even Moses ran out of time.

In any case, from whatever perspective one reads Psalm 90, it is clearly a psalm about time. It features numerous time words, and it is brutally honest about the limited time allotted to human beings. Even so, Psalm 90 is not finally pessimistic or despairing or hopeless. After the turning point that occurs in verses 11–12— the question and the request for wisdom—the psalm concludes on a note that is quite positive and promising, inviting us human beings to view our limited time and limited possibilities from the larger perspective of God's unlimited time (vv. 1–2, 4) and God's ability to "prosper the work of our hands" (v. 17) in a way that we ourselves cannot do.

Dimensions of Meaning

Title

As suggested above, the attribution of Psalm 90 to Moses seems more than coincidental at this point in the Psalter. The title is not to be understood as an indication of Mosaic authorship. Rather, in response to the crisis of exile, it seems that the editors of the Psalter wanted to take the reader back to a Mosaic perspective. It is as if they imagined Psalm 90 as Moses' intercession for the people in a manner similar to the way that Moses had interceded for the people in an earlier crisis—the golden calf episode (compare Ps. 90:13 with Exod. 32:12, where Moses tells God to "turn from your fierce wrath"). Moses is also called "the man of God" in Deuteronomy 33:1, the introduction of Moses' blessing of the people shortly before he died.

Verses 1–2

Before turning sustained attention to humanity and its allotted time, the psalmist focuses squarely on God and God's time. The very first words of the psalm address God as "Lord," and the divine name "God" concludes verse 2. Thus, this opening section is framed by references to God, as if to suggest that God's presence is all-encompassing, surrounding humanity and the entire created order "from everlasting to everlasting." The pronoun "you" in verse 1 is given emphasis by the Hebrew syntax. While everything else may be uncertain, God has been and is a reliable "dwelling place." This affirmation is probably best known in the words of Isaac Watts's metrical paraphrase of Psalm 90:

> O God, our help in ages past,
> Our hope for years to come,
> Our shelter from the stormy blast,
> And our eternal home.

Although the assurance of verses 1–2 seems to wane in verses 3–10, it is revived in verses 13–17. Thus, in terms of the psalm's larger structure, doubt and uncertainly are encompassed by faith and assurance. Trust in God and in the expansive reality of God's time means that the passage of human time is not simply reason for hopelessness and despair.

Verses 3–10

The transience of human time and the impermanence of human accomplishment are immediately in view in verse 3 as it alludes to

Genesis 2:7 and 3:19—that is, the creature formed from the ground returns to the dust. Time words and phrases occur repeatedly in this section of the psalm: "years" (vv. 4, 9, 10), "yesterday" (v. 4), "watch in the night" (v. 4), "morning" (vv. 5, 6), "evening" (v. 6), "days" (vv. 9, 10). In fact, the poetic content and structure of verses 5–6 effectively reproduce the passage of time, moving from night (v. 5a), to morning (vv. 5b–6a), and back to "evening" (v. 6). The grass imagery in verses 5–6 connects with Isaiah 40:6–8, a text from the exile (see also Ps. 103:15–16). As in Isaiah 40:6–8 and Psalm 90:1–2, the reader is reminded that human time and God's time are not the same (v. 4).

Verse 7 introduces the matter of God's "anger (see also v. 11) and "wrath" (a synonymous Hebrew word for "wrath" also occurs in vv. 9 and 11), and verses 7–10 clearly indicate a relationship among human sin, divine wrath, and human mortality. In this regard, like verse 3, verses 7–10 recall the opening chapters of the book of Genesis. The traditional reading of Genesis (and Ps. 90) concludes that human sin angered God and that, consequently, God punished humankind with mortality—that is, sin caused death. But the matter is more complicated than this. A closer reading of Genesis reveals that God punished sin by banishing Adam and Eve from the garden (Gen. 3:23), so it is better to conclude that mortality is an inherent dimension of being human (as opposed to being divine). From this perspective, while sin evokes God's wrath, God's wrath does not lead God to punish humanity by imposing on it mortality. In short, Adam and Eve, the representative humans, would have died even if they had not sinned. Such a conclusion invites us to consider the significance of God's wrath in a way that is different from the traditional reading of Genesis 1–3 and Psalm 90. James Mays's explanation of the significance of divine wrath in Psalm 90 is helpful:

> The wrath of God is a linguistic symbol for the divine limits and pressure placed against human resistance to his sovereignty. . . . Eternity belongs to the sovereign deity of the LORD as God. . . . Death is the final and ultimate "no" that cancels any pretension to autonomy from the human side.[1]

From this perspective, sin does not cause physical death. Rather, physical death is characteristic of humanity, just as eternity is characteristic of God. Death demonstrates to us that we are not divine, and the reality of death invites us to entrust life and future, including our own mortality, to God. When we resist such limitation and thus refuse the invitation to trust God, then mortality is experienced not as a natural part of the life cycle but rather as something to be denied and compensated for by our own pretentious self-assertion. In this case, one can conclude that death—or more precisely, the denial of and/or fear of death—causes sin!

Thus, one should not conclude from verse 10 that human life is inevitably filled with nothing but "toil and trouble." To be sure, life inevitably contains difficulties, and in comparison to God's eternity, our lives are painfully short—our days are "soon gone, and we fly away." But for those who entrust life and future to God, there is more to life than the experience of God's wrath; there is more than "toil and trouble." Thus, after a further acknowledgment of God's anger and wrath (v. 11), the psalmist requests in verse 12 the wisdom to live in a way that will make joy and gladness a possibility (vv. 13–17, especially v. 15).

Verses 11–12

Quite appropriately, Hossfeld and Zenger conclude that verses 11–12 are "the center of the psalm," functioning as a "link," or "hinge," or "turning point."[2] As we have seen, the repetition of "anger" and "wrath" links this center to verses 3–10, and verse 12 is more of an actual "turning point." If the experience of God's anger or wrath were all that is possible for human life, it would be rather cruel for the psalmist to pray, "So teach us to count our days." This fact, plus the subsequent mention of "a wise heart," as well as the more hope-filled content of verses 13–17, suggest that verse 12 is indeed a "turning point."

But what is the precise meaning of the request in verse 12? Checking off the days on a calendar is clearly not the point. James Limburg cites Martin Luther's rendering of verse 12, "Teach us to reflect on the fact that we must die, so that we become wise."

Then, borrowing from Luther, Limburg offers an expanded paraphrase: "Lord, teach us to make each day count, to reflect on the fact that we must die, and so become wise."[3] The psalmist seems to be praying for the wisdom to value fully each day of life, and so to live to the fullest every day. It is revealing, especially in view of the mention of sin, wrath, and mortality in verses 3–11, that the psalmist prays not for forgiveness or for immortality but for this sort of wisdom. As Hossfeld and Zenger put it:

> [The psalmist] petitions for a right wisdom about life, an ability to deal with the knowledge of death in such a way— beyond all categories, such as divine wrath or death as punishment for sin—that life can be accepted as a gift from God and lived as something fulfilled. Thus the petitioner asks that knowing about the limitedness of the time allotted to each person may make one aware of the immense value of every single day . . . , the *now* given one at each and every moment.[4]

The importance of living to the fullest in "the now" is reinforced when verse 12 is heard in a Mosaic context—in particular, the story of the manna in the wilderness that seems to be alluded to in verse 14 by way of the petition "Satisfy us in the morning." In Exodus 16, the Israelites were, in essence, satisfied every morning by God's provision of manna, which could not be hoarded because it lasted only one day. It is interesting that the Hebrew consonants in the word "manna" are the same as in the verb "count" in Psalm 90:12, perhaps another little clue that we are to hear verse 12 in in terms of living in "the now." An apt paraphrase of verse 12—one that complements Luther's and Limburg's—may be "Teach us to live day by day," or "Teach us to live one day at a time." In short, to receive our allotted time as a gift from God and to live our lives to the fullest every single day is what a "wise heart" is all about.

Verses 13–17

The opening petition of verse 13, "Turn, O LORD!" recalls verse 3, and the contrast between verses 13 and 3 again signals that a transition has occurred. Whereas God's turning in verse 3 had negative connotations, here in verse 13 the direction is much more positive—God's turning is associated with "compassion" for God's "servants" (see Deut. 32:36). Subsequent verses make clear what God's "compassion," along with God's "steadfast love" (v. 14), will mean for God's people and for human existence. Beyond "toil and trouble" (v. 10), there is the possibility for satisfaction (v. 14), joy (v. 14), and gladness (vv. 14–15). It is to be noted that several of the same time words from verses 3–10 are present as well in verses 13–17—"morning" (v. 14), "days" (vv. 14, 15), "years" (v. 15)—but now the possibilities for experiencing the passage of time are much more positive. In short, those persons who "gain a wise heart" (v. 12) will receive life as a gift, will entrust their days and years to God, and will experience the passage of time as something more than burdensome, oppressive, and depressing. When our time is viewed from the perspective of God's time, when we are open to the experience of God's "compassion" (v. 13) and "steadfast love" (v. 14), when we trust life and future to God, then God sets us free to live one day at a time, claiming "the now" as God's gift as we make each day count. Such is the foundation of genuine satisfaction, gladness, and joy.

Although English translations regularly obscure it, the repetition of "children" in verses 3 and 16 also marks the psalmist's transformed understanding of time. Verse 3 reads more literally, "Turn back, you children of humanity." The birth and growth of children is, of course, an important way in which we human beings mark the passage of time. In verse 3, "children" are associated with human transience. But in verse 16, the petition is for God to make "manifest . . . your glorious power to their children." Here "children" are associated with the perception of God's "work" (v. 16), and even beyond this, it seems that God's "glorious power" can "prosper [or "establish," NIV] the work of our hands" (v. 17). Yes, the span of even the longest human life is short (v. 10), and yes, human institutions and structures crumble with time, but by looking to God and living for God day by day, we human beings participate in and contribute constructively to something greater than ourselves and our own accomplishments.

The phrase "glorious power" in verse 16 translates a Hebrew word associated elsewhere with the proclamation of God's reign (see "majesty" in Pss. 29:4; 96:6), and the intimation of God's reign is suggestive. In short, when we entrust life and future to God, "the work of our hands" contributes to God's "work"—that is, the reign or realm of God. The final stanza of Purd Deitz's eloquent hymn, "We Would Be Building," captures well the essence of the psalmist's request in verses 16–17:

> O keep us building, Savior;
> may our hands ne'er falter when the dream is in our hearts,
> when to our ears there come divine commands and all the
>   pride of sinful will departs.
> We build with you;
> O grant enduring worth until your promised realm shall come
>   on earth.[5]

Psalm 90 for Today

For most people today, at least in North America, time and its passing seem to be an enemy. A recent ad for a high-tech stopwatch features the following copy: "See the Enemy. Time is taunting you like a loudmouth jerk. . . . You can't outrun Time if you can't see Time." For most of us, the first line of the ad says it all— time is "the Enemy." Of course, the ad goes on to imply that we *can* outrun time (if we buy the stopwatch), but we finally cannot outrun time, as Psalm 90 so poignantly reminds us: our "days . . . are soon gone, and we fly away" (v. 10).

Even young children know the truth of this statement. When my great-aunt died, my wife and I tried to explain to our two little children, ages four and two, why we would never be able to see Aunt Lucy again. Since that time, each one knows enough to say occasionally, "I miss Lucy!" And the four-year-old will say from time to time, "Daddy, I don't want to die." The very fact that she says such a thing indicates that she already knows she will die someday. I tell her that I do not want to die either, and that I hope she will live a long time, but that someday we all will die. Biblically speaking, such knowledge is the foundation for a wise heart, a heart intent upon entrusting life and future to God, and upon living life to the fullest every day.

But in a contemporary culture in which time is seen as the enemy, it is difficult to "gain a wise heart." In our culture, the better part of wisdom seems to involve denial of the aging process and, at least implicitly, the denial of death, even when we know better—thus the popularity of hair dye, treatments for baldness, Botox injections, and cosmetic surgery. To be sure, these strategies are not inherently wrong or morally objectionable, but they almost certainly do not help us, in Luther's words, "to reflect on the fact that we must die."

Yes, this is a sad and painful fact, as Psalm 90 recognizes, but it does not preclude, as Psalm 90 also recognizes and affirms, the genuine experience of satisfaction, gladness, and joy. As John Goldingay concludes concerning Psalm 39, another psalm that recognizes the brevity of human life (see especially Ps. 39:4–6), "It invites us to live life in light of the fact that we are on our way to death—which does not imply living in gloom and fear but making the most of every day, because we know our days will not last for long."[6] When we entrust ourselves to God, including our living and our dying, then the reality of death will draw us more fully into life. We will be impelled to make every day count. In this same direction, the book of Ecclesiastes even affirms the following in 7:2:

> It is better to go to the house of mourning
>   than to go to the house of feasting;
> for this is the end of everyone,
>   and the living will lay it to heart.

I have never met another pastor who would rather do a wedding than a funeral (although I am sure that there are some). It is not because we pastors are morbid people, or because we think funerals are fun. Rather, funerals virtually force us "to reflect on the fact that we must die," and because they do, they invite us to "gain a wise heart," to discern what is truly important in life, and so to live life to the fullest each day.

Biblically speaking, to live life to the fullest means quite literally to live for God's sake, which in turn means living in community with all God's people toward a future entrusted to God. Therein lies the promise of the satisfaction, gladness, and joy anticipated in verses 13–17. The following words of Reinhold Niebuhr eloquently express this promise:

> Nothing that is worth doing can be achieved in our lifetime; therefore we must be saved by hope. Nothing which is true or beautiful or good makes complete sense in any immediate context of history; therefore we must be saved by faith. Nothing we do, however virtuous, can be accomplished alone; therefore we must be saved by love. No virtuous act is quite as virtuous from the standpoint of our friend or foe as it is from our standpoint. Therefore, we must be saved by the final form of love which is forgiveness.[7]

In the final analysis, Psalm 90 is an invitation to throw ourselves upon God's "compassion" (v. 13) and "steadfast love" (v. 14), resolved to live by faith, hope, and love. Insofar as we do, we shall realize the wisdom of the following words from the martyred archbishop of El Salvador, Oscar Romero—words that, like the concluding verses of Psalm 90, affirm the priority of God's work in the world, to which our work may contribute:

> It helps, now and then, to step back and take the long view.
> The Kingdom is not only beyond our efforts, it is even
> beyond our vision.
> We accomplish in our lifetime only a tiny fraction of the magnificent enterprise that is God's work.
> Nothing we do is complete, which is another way of saying that the Kingdom always lies beyond us. . . .
> This is what we are about.
> We plant the seeds that one day will grow.
> We water seeds already planted, knowing that they hold future promise.
> We lay foundations that will need further development.

We provide yeast that produces effects far beyond our capa-
bilities.
We cannot do everything; and there is a sense of liberation in
realizing that.
This enables us to do something, and to do it very well.
It may be incomplete, but it is a beginning, a step along the way,
an opportunity for the Lord's grace to enter and do the rest.
We may never see the end results, but that is the difference
between the master builder and the worker.
We are workers, not master builders, ministers, not messiahs.
We are prophets of a future that is not our own.[8]

Indeed! And so we pray with the psalmist, "O prosper the work of
our hands!"

Questions for Reflection and Discussion

1. The preceding comments on Psalm 90 suggest that the
   psalm is honest and realistic but not hopeless or depressing. Do you agree? How do you hear Psalm 90?
2. A recent sociological study concluded that older people
   are generally happier than younger people. Might this be
   due to their increased time for reflection on the certainty
   of death? In any case, how have your understandings of
   living and dying changed as you have grown older?
3. Despite increasing life expectancies and the aging of the
   population of the United States, we still seem to live in a
   culture that glorifies youth and youthful appearance. Is
   denial of aging and dying involved in all this? What might
   we be missing?
4. Psalm 90:16–17 invites attention to both God's work and
   human work, and Oscar Romero suggests that realizing
   that "we cannot do everything" frees us "to do something,
   and to do it very well." What thing can you do very well
   that may contribute "a tiny fraction" to "the magnificent
   enterprise that is God's work"?
5. How might we best teach children about death and dying,
   and what might we learn from them?

Chapter Ten

Psalm 103

The opening line of Psalm 103 is among the most familiar in the book of Psalms, and Psalm 103 as a whole is well-known and loved. As James Limburg puts it, "Few psalms have had the impact of Psalm 103."[1] Perhaps at least part of the reason that Psalm 103 has had such an impact is that it aims to be comprehensive in expressing God's claim upon human life and the life of the world. Notice that Psalm 103 moves from an initial focus on the individual person ("O my soul" in vv. 1–2) to give attention to Israel (vv. 7–13), then to humanity as a whole (vv. 11–18), and finally to the entire creation (vv. 19–22). The twenty-two verses of the psalm match the number of letters in the Hebrew alphabet, again suggesting that Psalm 103 intends to say it all. Indeed, in this regard, another noticeable stylistic feature of Psalm 103 is the repetition of the word "all," especially at the beginning and end of the psalm (see vv. 1–3, 6, 19, 21–22), reinforcing the articulation of the breadth of God's claim—God's "kingdom rules over all" (v. 19), so God is to be praised by "all his works" in "all places of his dominion" (v. 22).

Another probable reason for the major impact of Psalm 103 is its proclamation that the universally sovereign God exercises God's governance of the world mercifully and lovingly. The two key words in Psalm 103 occur for the first time in verse 4—"steadfast love" and "mercy." Each will be repeated three more times—

"steadfast love" in verses 8, 11, and 17, and forms of "mercy" in v. 8 (NRSV, "merciful") and twice in v. 13 (NRSV, "compassion"). In particular, the occurrences of "steadfast love" pervade the psalm, and the final two occurrences emphasize the virtually infinite extent of God's love. As Konrad Schaefer concludes, "How can what was essentially clay not respond to a love of such grand dimensions, as high as the sky, which removes sin as far as east is from west and whose tenderness and affection are as profound as a mother's and a father's for their little children."[2]

Psalm 103 is in Book IV of the Psalter, and as we saw in the previous chapter on Psalm 90, Book IV seems designed to respond to the crisis of exile by returning the reader to a Mosaic perspective. In this regard, it is probably not coincidental that Psalm 102:12–22 speaks of Zion as in need of "compassion" (v. 13) and rebuilding. In this context, Psalm 103 functions to articulate the praise anticipated by Psalm 102 (see especially vv. 15, 18, 21–22). In any case, Psalm 103 specifically mentions Moses (v. 7), and the two key words mentioned above—"steadfast love" and "mercy" or "compassion"—are featured in God's self-revelation to Moses in Exodus 34:6–7. Furthermore, the celebration of God's gracious willingness to forgive is reminiscent of the exilic/postexilic portions of the book of Isaiah. It is not surprising that there are several similarities between Psalm 103 and Isaiah 40–55 (for example, compare v. 5 with Isa. 40:31; v. 9 with Isa. 57:16; v. 11 with Isa. 55:9; vv. 15–16 with Isa. 40:6–8; ar note that "steadfast love" is mentioned in Isa. 54:10 and 55:3, "mercy" or "compassion" are mentioned in Isa. 49:10, 13; 5⁴ 10; 55:7), not the least of which is that both affirm God's v sovereignty (see Ps. 103:19–22; Isa. 52:7–10).

In this direction, Psalm 104 continues the portrar world-encompassing claim, and, of course, it is n' Psalms 103 and 104 are explicitly connected by w' tical opening and closing line, "Bless the LORD, ' ally, Psalm 104 concludes by adding *hallelujah* Somewhat surprisingly, this is the first instan' Psalter, and as James L. Mays observes, "Co ate place be found?"[3]

Dimensions of Meaning

Verses 1–5

The invitations to "bless the LORD" or bless God's "name" in the opening two verses anticipate the four invitations to "bless" in verses 20–22. Thus, the concept of blessing God encompasses the psalm. The verb "bless" seems originally to have meant "to kneel," connoting subservience or submission to a sovereign (see Pss. 16:7; 26:12; 34:1; 63:4; 95:6; 96:2; 100:4; 145:1, 21). The pattern of repetition reinforces the importance of the proclamation of the world-encompassing claim of God.

The Hebrew word translated "soul" means more accurately the whole self, life, or being. The psalmist poetically requests his or her whole self to submit to God's claim, and the first occurrence of "all" reinforces the notion of complete devotion to God. The mention of God's "name" calls to mind God's character, which is more fully described in verses 8–17. But already in this opening section, God's characteristic activity is in view (vv. 3–5). Verses 3–5 are introduced as God's "benefits." The Hebrew word underlying "benefits" most frequently elsewhere designates something negative—retribution or punishment (see v. 10, where "repay" translates the same Hebrew root). In an apparent play on words, the psalmist proclaims the good news that God's "retribution" involves things such as forgiveness (v. 3a), healing (v. 3b), redemption (v. 4a), merciful love (v. 4b), satisfaction (v. 5a), and renewal (v. 5b)! Not surprisingly, several of these terms appear elsewhere in both Mosaic and exilic contexts, suggesting that Psalm 103 would have been an apt response to the crisis of exile—for instance, see "forgive" and "forgiveness" in Exodus 34:9 and Isaiah 55:7; "heals" and "healing" in Exodus 15:26 and Isaiah 57:18; "edeems" in Exodus 6:6, 15:13, Isaiah 43:1, 44:22–23, and 51:10; d "satisfies" and "satisfaction" in Exodus 16:8, 12, and Isa 58:11.

Verse 6

ranslations suggest a break between verses 5 and 6, but the
f participles featured in verses 3–5 continues in verse 6, so it

could properly be construed as the concluding and climactic element in the list of God's "benefits." This would make good sense, because "righteousness" (NIV; NRSV, "vindication") and "justice" serve elsewhere as a summary of what God characteristically wills and works for in the world (see Pss. 9:7–8; 89:14; 96:13; 97:2; 98:9; 99:4; note that several of these contexts explicitly affirm God's world-encompassing sovereignty, which is also in view in Ps. 103). On the other hand, the participle in verse 6 ("works") is the only one in verses 3–6 that has a subject ("LORD"), so the grammatical construction is somewhat different from that of verses 3–5, perhaps signaling a new section of the psalm. Given the ambiguity, it may be best to see verse 6 as a transitional verse, both concluding the series of participles found in verses 3–5 and anticipating the allusions to Moses and the exodus from Egypt in verse 7 and the following verses. The adjective "oppressed" in verse 6 is used in Isaiah 52:4 to describe the people's condition during the Egyptian captivity.

Verses 7–18

The articulation in verse 6 of God's characteristic activity—righteousness and justice—is a prelude to the focus on God's character in verses 7–18. The mention of Moses in verse 7 recalls both the exodus event (see "his acts" in v. 7b) and the whole Sinai experience (see "his ways" in v. 7a), a particular episode of which is explicitly in view in verse 8—namely, God's self-revelation to Moses (Exod. 34:6–7) toward the conclusion of the golden calf episode (Exod. 32–34; see the chapter on Ps. 51). In fact, verse 8 is a slightly abbreviated form of Exodus 34:6, which functions in the Old Testament as something like a creed (see Pss. 86:15; 111:4; 145:8). It affirms that God is essentially gracious, and verses 9–13 are an elaboration upon this theme, concluding with three similes in verses 11–13. The first (v. 11) and third (v. 13) feature respectively the two key words of the psalm, "steadfast love" and "mercy" or "compassion," both of which occur in the creed-like statement in verse 8.

The similes move from the most distant ("as the heavens are high above the earth") to the most intimate ("as a father has compassion for his children"). The word "compassion" occurs twice in verse 13. Although the "compassion" here is associated explicitly with a father, the word itself appears to have a decidedly maternal dimension. A noun form of the Hebrew root means "womb," suggesting that the form of the word that appears in verse 13 should more properly be understood as something like "motherly compassion" or "womb-love."[4] In any case, God is characterized as a parent who can do nothing other than mercifully, compassionately love her or his children, despite their "sins" (v. 10), "iniquities" (v. 10), and "transgressions" (v. 12; see Hos. 11:1–9; Luke 15:11–32; and the chapter on Ps. 51).

The emphasis on grace appears to be compromised by the qualification that "steadfast love" and "compassion" are for "those who fear him" (vv. 11, 13, 17). But "fear" here should not be understood as something that earns God's love. Rather, "fear" connotes faith or trust—that is, it communicates essentially the willingness to accept forgiveness and thus to live by grace. Those who accept God's grace will live in relationship to God—that is, they will "keep his covenant" (v. 18)—and despite their sinfulness (vv. 10, 12), they will "remember to do his commandments" (v. 18). In essence, the mention of "fear" is an indication that grace is not cheap or ineffectual; rather, it claims us and orients us to God and to doing God's will.

Verses 19–22

The final section of the psalm clearly recalls its opening section by way of the fourfold repetition of "bless," as well as the threefold repetition of "all." Eventually, of course, the final line of Psalm 103 repeats its opening line. But before the psalmist concludes by inviting himself or herself again to "bless the LORD," the invitation to bless God is extended to a universe-encompassing congregation: God's "angels," "mighty ones," "all his hosts," "his ministers," and "all his works." This expansive congregation matches the extent of God's sovereignty—"his kingdom rules over all" (v. 19). The affirmation of God's universal sovereignty accords well with one of the primary emphases of Book IV of the Psalter (see the chapter on Ps. 90), and verse 19 recalls Psalm 93, the first psalm in the enthronement collection (see "throne" in v. 19 and Ps. 93:2).

As we have seen, the creationwide perspective of verses 19–22 anticipates Psalm 104, which is linked to Psalm 103 by the opening and closing, "Bless the LORD, O my soul." In particular, "all his works" (v. 22) are in view in Psalm 104 (see "work" or "works" in Ps. 104:13, 24a; the verb "make" or "makes" in vv. 4, 19, and 24b represents the same Hebrew root). By placing himself or herself in the universe-encompassing congregation of verses 19–22, the psalmist suggests that submission to God and God's will is what puts human beings in touch with and in harmony with the entire cosmos God has created and claims as God's own. Both the theological and the ecological implications are profound and far-reaching (see the chapters on Pss. 8 and 148).

Psalm 103 for Today

Artur Weiser summarizes the message of Psalm 103 by saying that the psalmist "has been granted an insight into the heart of the majesty of God, and what he found there is grace."[5] Several of our previous psalms have given us the opportunity to think about and talk about grace (see Pss. 13, 23, 32, 51), but in our thoroughly merit-oriented society, we Christians should probably take advantage of every opportunity to think and talk even further about grace. If we do not, we may be in danger of emptying the word "grace" of any theological content.

Indeed, this may already have happened. Several years ago when I was working on annotations of the Psalms for *The Learning Bible*, a project of the American Bible Society, I was discouraged to learn that the word "grace" was to be avoided in commenting upon the Psalms (and any other biblical book). Why? According to the directors of the project, the word "grace" is generally incomprehensible or almost inevitably misunderstood by most ordinary readers. Their reader surveys showed that "grace" communicates to most people something having to do with physical movement, beauty, or charm—that is, a dancer or ice skater moves with grace, and an actress or even a luxury car may possess grace.[6] In short, if we Christians want to retain "grace" as a meaningful theological word, we are going to have to think and talk more carefully about it, and help others to do so as well. Perhaps Psalm 103 can help.

In his volume *Elements of Old Testament Theology*, Claus Westermann initiates his treatment of divine compassion with a discussion of Psalm 103. His conclusions concerning the psalm and its message may help us understand and communicate to others the meaning of grace:

> The poet has no intention of contesting God's activity in wrath. But he makes a distinction. God's activity in wrath is limited; God's goodness knows no boundaries (v. 17). . . . The same is true of sin and forgiveness. If God compensated man commensurate with the way he sins, then one might despair. But here too, God is inconsistent; his forgiving goodness is immeasurable. One might even say that the entire psalm deals with the incomprehensible excess of God's goodness.[7]

Grace involves "the incomprehensible excess of God's goodness." Despite God's fervent desire that people obediently join God at God's work of setting things right in the world—that is, justice and righteousness (v. 6)—and despite the incessant human refusal to do so, God simply cannot and will not let people go. God's wrath communicates God's disappointment, displeasure, and pain, but God never refuses to forgive.

The third and climactic simile in verses 11–13—the parental image—may be particularly apt, for we human parents often know as well the agony of dealing with wayward children, whom we love without limits and will never simply let go. Psalm 103, especially verse 13, anticipates Jesus' parable of the Prodigal Son, or as it is better titled, the parable of the Loving Father (Luke 15:11–32). All the prodigal son has to do to receive forgiveness is ask for it and accept it. Like Psalm 103, the parable affirms that God's "forgiving goodness is immeasurable." In short, psalm and parable alike affirm that God is essentially gracious. As the reaction of the older brother in the parable illustrates (Luke 15:25–32), the "excess of God's goodness" seems to have been as incomprehensible then as it is now. After all, grace is not fair. But to those who are honest enough to admit that they are sinners, grace is good news—indeed, the best news possible (see the chapter on Pss. 32 and 51).

With good reason, Erhard Gerstenberger concludes that Psalm 103 "exhibits a lot of pastoral care."[8] Insofar as it was designed to address defeated and dispirited exiles, who seemingly had lost every sign and symbol of meaning, perhaps as a result of their own rebellious behavior (as the prophets had warned), Psalm 103 promises that life and future are still possible, due not to the resilience of the human spirit but to the incomprehensible excess of God's goodness. To us contemporary folk, who often have difficulty detecting any genuine and enduring meaning to our lives or the life of the world, Psalm 103 also promises that submission to God offers the possibility of putting our lives and our futures in harmony with all creation. As Konrad Schaefer concludes, "*Hesed* ["steadfast love"] endows the individual's life, the history of the people, even the cosmos with ultimate meaning."[9]

One of the words that the editors of *The Learning Bible* suggested as a contemporary substitute for "grace" was "acceptance," and this is actually a very good choice. In a world where so many people feel unacceptable, for whatever reason, or may have been told by others that they are unacceptable, the incomprehensible excess of God's goodness is good news indeed. No one is unacceptable in God's sight! This is grace!

Questions for Reflection and Discussion

1. We speak fairly frequently of being blessed by God, and we pray for God to bless us. Think further about the meaning and importance of our blessing God with our whole lives and selves. For instance, given the popularity of the song "God Bless America," what might it mean to say, in addition, "Bless God, America"?

2. The parental image in verse 13 is explicitly paternal, but

the word clearly has a maternal dimension. Why might it be important to think and talk about God as a compassionate mother as well as a compassionate father?

3. In addition to the parable of the Loving Father, another parable in which the contours of grace are particularly sharp is the parable of the Workers in the Vineyard (Matt. 20:1–16). When the laborers who worked only a short time get paid the same amount as those who worked all day long, the latter protest the landowner's labor practices. The owner replies that he has not violated any agreements, and he asks the protesters, "Or are you envious because I am generous?" Clearly they are, and we too are often bothered by grace. Consider the unfairness of grace and how you are inclined to respond to "the incomprehensible excess of God's goodness."

4. Given the apparent lack of a theological understanding of the word "grace" in our contemporary cultural context, what associations or thoughts come to mind when you hear the word "grace"? Is "acceptance" a helpful alternative? Why or why not? Can you think of other possibilities?

5. We will have the opportunity to consider this further in the chapter on Psalm 148, but what might it mean now for us to bless God with our whole selves in community with "all his works" (v. 22)?

Chapter Eleven

Psalm 139

Despite verses 19–22, which Erhard Gerstenberger suggests "seem to be disgustingly inferior to the noble, humble, and open kind of thinking presented in vv. 1–18,"[1] Psalm 139 is a very popular psalm. It appears four times in the Revised Common Lectionary (although the lectionary excludes vv. 19–22 in each case), and Psalm 139 has been frequently studied in detail by biblical scholars as well. Konrad Schaefer's assessment of Psalm 139 may explain in large part why it is so popular: "The remarkable feature of this poem is the sense of intimacy with God."[2]

This sense of intimacy with God is communicated clearly by the key word in Psalm 139—"know(n)" or "knowledge," which occurs seven times (vv. 1, 2, 4, 6, 14, and twice in v. 23). Since seven is the biblical number of completion, and since the word "know" communicates elsewhere a relationship as intimate as sexual intercourse, the sevenfold repetition communicates the psalmist's conviction that he or she is fully and intimately known by God. The fact that "know(n)" occurs twice again in verse 23 also means that this concept frames the poem, again reinforcing the importance of a sense of intimacy with God.

The two occurrences of "know" in verse 23 are both imperatives, inviting God's continuing relationship with or even penetrating examination of the psalmist and his or her thinking and acting. Most commentators suggest that verses 23–24, along with verses 19–22, are the most likely clue to the origin and ancient use of Psalm 139—namely, the psalmist had been falsely accused by those who are called "the wicked" (v. 19a), "the bloodthirsty" (v. 19b), and the "enemies" (v. 21). In order to affirm his or her innocence, the psalmist emphasized the sense of intimacy with God (vv. 1–18, 23–24), and at the same time the psalmist thoroughly distanced himself or herself from the accusers (vv. 19–22), whom the psalmist described not only as his or her own enemies but also as opponents of God (vv. 20–21).

While this proposal may well be correct (see also Pss. 7, 17, 26), it is clear that Psalm 139 has served the people of God in situations other than false accusation. Because it is in Book V (Pss. 107–150), which along with Book IV (Pss. 90–106) seems to be designed to respond to the crisis of exile and its aftermath (see the chapter on Psalm 90), Psalm 139 may have served to help the post-exilic community express its conviction of God's ongoing presence with God's people, despite continuing setback and persecution. But beyond this possibility, Psalm 139 has articulated for many generations of Jews and Christians a profound sense of intimacy with God.

Dimensions of Meaning

Verses 1–6

Four of the seven occurrences of "know(n)" or "knowledge" are in this opening section of the psalm (vv. 1, 2, 4, 6), effectively making the point that the psalmist is fully and intimately known by God. In the Hebrew as well as in the NRSV, the very first word in the psalm is the divine name, and the pronoun "you" that begins verse 2 is emphatic—that is, the psalmist unambiguously affirms that *God knows me* in every possible way. The various life-settings the psalmist mentions are meant to be comprehensive: sitting down and rising up (v. 2), thinking (v. 2), lifestyle (see "my paths" in v. 3a and "all my ways" in v. 3b), and speaking (v. 4). The repetition of "all" (v. 3b; NRSV, "completely" in v. 4b) reinforces the sense of complete intimacy—God knows everything about the psalmist and his or her life.

As verse 5 at least begins to hint, such intimate knowledge on God's part could be perceived as threatening. In other contexts, the verb "hem in" often has a negative connotation, indicating captivity or oppression. As Gerstenberger suggests, the psalmist could rightly worry that God's pervasive supervision amounts to something like "Big Brother is watching you."[3] But verse 6 indicates that the psalmist perceives God's constant presence and intimate knowledge as liberating rather than limiting. The adjective translated "wonderful" represents a Hebrew root that is used elsewhere to describe the exodus (see "wonders" in Exod. 3:20) and other acts of divine deliverance (see "marvelous" in Ps. 118:23). This Hebrew root can also suggest incomprehensibility, as verse 6b seems to suggest. Even so, it affirms that the incredible knowledge God possesses is liberating and life-serving, not threatening or harmful.

Verses 7–12

Despite the clearly positive direction of verse 6, Gerstenberger characterizes the question that begins verse 7 as a "terrorized rhetorical question."[4] He finds support for this conclusion in the fact that the verb "flee" ordinarily communicates an attempt to escape from something or someone. Here it would be the attempt to escape God's "presence," or more literally, "face." The word "spirit" also suggests God's presence (see Gen. 1:2; see also Isa. 63:9–10, where "spirit" and "face" occur in the same context). Then too, verses 7–10 are quite similar to Amos 9:2–4, and in this latter text, the reality of God's inescapable presence is unambiguously bad news.

But if Gerstenberger is correct, the terror quickly subsides and is replaced by trust. The verbs "lead" and "hold" occur together in Psalm 73:23–24, clearly communicating assurance (NRSV, "guide" in 73:24), and the verb "lead" especially indicates God's gracious guidance (see Pss. 5:8; 23:3; 27:11; 31:3; 43:3; 61:2; and 143:10, where the request is that God's "spirit" may "lead" the psalmist). So God's presence is ultimately not a threat but a promise. It is good news, perhaps even unprecedented good news, since the psalmist affirms that God is present even "in Sheol" (v. 8). The traditional view of Sheol permitted God no access (see Job 17:12– 16; Pss. 6:5; 30:3, 9; 88:3–7), although there are a couple more instances in the Psalms where the poets at least seem to imagine that God can somehow reach the realm of the dead (Pss. 22:29; 49:14–15).

Verses 11–12 also suggest that terror no longer prevails. What would normally be a threat—that is, "dark(ness)," which occurs four times in verses 11–12 (see also Job 12:22; 17:12–13; Pss. 23:4; 88:6, 12, 18)—is transformed by God into something positively good. Elsewhere in the Old Testament, "light" serves to characterize God's "presence" or "face" (see Num. 6:25–26; Pss. 4:6; 27:1, 8–9; 44:3; 89:15). So at this point, verses 11–12 allude to verse 7, and the language and imagery of verses 11–12 also anticipate the affirmation found in John 1:15: "The light shines in the darkness, and the darkness did not overcome it."

Verses 13–18

Recalling verse 2, verse 13 begins in Hebrew with an emphatic "you," reinforcing the focus on God's active knowledge of the psalmist. Or, from the psalmist's perspective, the sense of intimacy with God is not only a present experience but also extends to the past (vv. 13–16a) and to the future (v. 16b). While the psalmist is talking about his or her own origin or creation in verses 13–16a, it is appropriate to draw more general conclusions about human life. In particular, verses 13–16a affirm that the origin of each human life is not simply the result of familiar biological processes. Rather, each human life is a divine gift, for which God is to be praised or thanked (the verb translated "praise" in v. 14 is often translated "thank"). In short, human life is to be received with gratitude as a gift from God. John Calvin's comment on Psalm 22:9 would also be appropriate here:

> Although it is by the operation of natural causes that infants come into the world, and are nourished with their mother's

milk, yet therein the wonderful providence of God brightly shines forth. This miracle, it is true, because of its ordinary occurrence, is made less account of by us. But if ingratitude did not put upon our eyes the veil of stupidity, we would be ravished with admiration at every childbirth in the world.[5]

To be "ravished with admiration" is communicated in Psalm 139 by the clause "for I am fearfully and wonderfully made" (v. 14). The translation "fearfully" is not necessarily inaccurate, but it may be misleading. In more contemporary English, we might say, "I am awesomely . . . made." The word "wonderful" that begins verse 14b recalls the occurrence of "wonderful" in verse 6. The juxtaposition of the exclamation "Wonderful are your works" with the poetic description of the psalmist's birth in verses 13–14a and 15–16a makes the daring claim that the ongoing reproduction of the human species belongs in the sequence of God's saving acts or mighty deeds! God values every single human being.

The poetic description of the psalmist's birth in verse 13 does not employ the more familiar metaphor of God as potter (see Gen. 2:7; Jer. 18:11) but rather portrays God as a weaver, who has "knit . . . together" the psalmist (see Job 10:11). Although the Hebrew words differ, "knit" may suggest some congruence between the metaphor in verse 13 and the creative process described in verses 15–16, where "woven" occurs. Even so, much remains elusive about verses 15–16. Why, for instance, does the process take place "in the depths of the earth"? Is this an allusion to some ancient Near Eastern mythic accounts in which people originated underground, or is "depths of the earth" a poetic image for the mother's womb? The answer is unclear, but apparently God is not ignorant of or absent from whatever process is being described.

Psalm 139 often appears in literature related to the topic of abortion, because of verse 13 and because of the Hebrew word translated "unformed substance" (v. 16). This translation is quite uncertain, since this Hebrew word occurs only this one time in the Old Testament, and since the process being described is not clear. In any case, the poetic language of verses 13–16 (and perhaps even mythic language in verses 15–16) clearly does not settle the scientific questions frequently posed in the debates about abortion. It is equally clear, however, that verses 13–16 are not devoid of ethical significance. On the whole, verses 13 and 15–16 support what verse 14 affirms more directly—that each human life is to be received as a gift from God and is to be valued accordingly.

Verse 16b, in which the future is in view, is not about God's predetermined plan for peoples' lives. Rather, the image of God's "book," in which "were written all the days that were formed for me," affirms poetically that the psalmist belongs to God in every way (concerning God's "book," see Exod. 32:32–33; Ps. 69:28; Mal. 3:16). If we take seriously that every human life originates from and belongs to God, there will be profound implications!

Verses 17–18 recall verse 2. While God is able to discern human thoughts, humans are overwhelmed by the prospect of even trying to measure God's thoughts. But such an attempt is not necessary. All that really matters to the psalmist about God is that she or he is "still with you" (see the chapter on Psalm 73). Thus, this section of the psalm concludes by featuring again what Schaefer calls "the sense of intimacy with God."

Verses 19–22

At this point, we arrive at the verses of the psalm that "seem to be disgustingly inferior" (recall Gerstenberger), so much so that many commentators conclude that this section was not a part of the original poem. As we have seen, the lectionary excludes verses 19–22 every time it employs Psalm 139. On the one hand, such editorial censorship is understandable—that is, we do not want to give the impression that the Bible sanctions hatred and violence, especially in a contemporary context where so much hatred and violence already exist. On the other hand, we should recognize that verses 19–22 are not at all unusual in the Psalms. By my count, there are fifty-seven instances in which the psalmist either requests God to dispose of his or her enemies, or celebrates the fact that God has done or will do so. So before excising verses 19–22 too quickly, perhaps we should consider more deeply the theological function of these verses, including how they might profitably and faithfully be appropriated in our violent world.[6]

If we take seriously the reality that the psalmist has been severely victimized—whether by being falsely accused or by some other way—then verses 19–22 become at least a bit more palatable. As C. S. Lewis suggests, the psalms that contain such vengeance elements show us "the natural result of injuring a human being."[7] That is, when people are hurt, they will lash out—indeed, they *should* lash out, at least verbally. The worst thing that can happen in the face of severe victimization is silence, which can easily pass for acquiescence or apathy. But the psalmists never remain silent. They give voice to their victimization, and such is the first step toward addressing and removing the threat.

Granted, we might wish that the psalmists sounded less revenge-oriented. But it is to be noted how the psalmist here (and the psalmists elsewhere) handle their natural feelings of revenge—that is, rather than acting them out, they entrust such feelings to God in prayer! In a real sense, then, these violent-sounding prayers actually break the cycle of violence. In other words, in the final analysis, verses 19–22 and similar requests and affirmations in the Psalms are *not* simply a matter of personal revenge. They are requests to God that God set things right in the life of the psalmist and in the life of the world—that is, they are prayers *for justice*. In fact, if we stay with such difficult texts long enough instead of censoring them immediately, we may even hear them whispering in the background, "Thy will be done." The psalmist's ultimate hope is that his or her intimacy with God will result in an end to victimization, and the psalmist's ultimate trust is that God will set things right. For those who are victimized, it is profound good news that God hates injustice, unrighteousness, and victimization. Indeed, we should hate such things as well.

Especially if the psalmist has been falsely accused, verses 19–22 can be heard as something like a loyalty oath (see Pss. 26:5; 31:6, NRSV note; 119:158). That is, the psalmist affirms emphatically both his or her innocence and unflinching loyalty to God and God's purposes, over against "the wicked" and "the bloodthirsty" (v. 19) and those who "rise up against" God (v. 21).

Verses 23–24

The psalmist's loyalty oath is rounded off nicely in verses 23–24, in which the psalmist asks God to do what verse 1 affirmed that God has done or is already doing—searching and knowing. As we have seen, the two occurrences of "know" in verse 23 make the total seven, and this number of fullness and completion clearly reinforces the sense of intimacy with God as the psalm concludes. The initial request of verse 24, "See," also picks up the language of verse 16 (NRSV, "behold"), another reinforcement of the conclusion that the psalmist desires to be, and is, fully known by God, an experience that borders on the eternal (v. 24; see 1 Cor. 13:12).

Psalm 139 for Today

James Limburg titles his treatment of Psalm 139 "Thank You for Me," explaining that one of his sons customarily included in his bedtime prayers not only thanks for all his family members but also "Thank you for me." Limburg appropriately suggests that this expression of gratitude captures the spirit of Psalm 139, communicating "healthy appreciation for the gift of life, . . . not just for life in general but for a specific, individual life."[8] In a contemporary context in which countless persons struggle with issues of self-worth and self-esteem, Psalm 139 affirms the good news that every one of us is "fearfully and wonderfully made" (v. 14).

Of course, a reality of our contemporary context is also that countless persons are told by others or by society that they are worthless, and the affirmation of life contained in Psalm 139 is pertinent in view of this sad reality as well. The scholarly proposal that Psalm 139 represents the ancient prayer of a falsely accused person may seem irrelevant to a contemporary appropriation of it, but recent studies have shown that false accusation—and even the carrying out of capital punishment in error—is all too prevalent in the justice system of the United States. But beyond the legal system itself, it is frequently the case that people are victimized—for example, the poor are often blamed for being poor and thus are doubly victimized both by being left out of the system and then being blamed for it. Blaming the poor for their plight is a

convenient excuse for not helping them, as well as for dehuman-
izing and devaluing them (and, of course, it is a convenient excuse
for not trying to change the system). A healthy appreciation for
the gift of life for all people is a much-needed perspective in our
world.

The reality of victimization also highlights the importance of
verses 19–22, the violent-sounding outburst of the victimized
psalmist. Beyond the suggestions already offered for not simply
rejecting verses 19–22 as morally inferior, it is the case that passages like this can provide an opportunity to talk about topics we
often prefer to avoid—victimization, vengeance, and violence. As
Walter Brueggemann concludes, we stand to learn something
about ourselves in the process:

> The real theological problem, I submit, is not that vengeance
> is *there* in the Psalms, but that it is *here* in our midst. And that
> it is there and here reflect how attuned the Psalter is to what
> goes on among us. Thus, we may begin with a recognition of
> the acute correspondence between what is *written there* and
> what is *practiced here*. The Psalms do "tell it like it is" with us.[9]

To be sure, verses 19–22 and similar texts in the Psalms are not to
be taken as biblical warrant for revenge, but the fact that the
psalmist takes his or her desire for vengeance to God in prayer is
instructive. What is legitimated is the necessity to name victimization and the recognition that we do have vengeful feelings.
What the psalmist models, however, is dealing with these feelings
in prayer rather than with a knife or a gun. People often speak of
the power of prayer, and if prayer were the primary means of dealing with our vengeful feelings, it would undoubtedly have a powerful effect toward reducing our national rates of violent crime.

To conclude, the key word in Psalm 139, "know(n)," plays a
central role in introducing the book of Psalms by way of its occurrence in Psalm 1:6: "for the LORD knows the way of the righteous"
(RSV). Of course, in Psalm 1, as well as in Psalm 139 (especially
vv. 19–22), "the wicked" are already a problem. And, in fact, Psalm
1:6 suggests that what the psalmist prays for in Psalm 139:19 will

become a reality: "but the way of the wicked will perish." The fact that the psalmist is still praying in Psalm 139 for what Psalm 1 affirmed is another reminder that the faithful life, then and now, inevitably incurs opposition (see the chapters on Pss. 13, 63, 73). So we contemporary people of faith still find ourselves praying the way the psalmist did in Psalm 139, articulating our sense of intimacy with God, entrusting ourselves fully to God, and asking God to set things right for us and for the world. No wonder that Psalm 139 remains such a popular psalm and a treasured theological resource, although as Patrick Miller points out, "it may translate into the poetic expression of Francis Thompson's 'The Hound of Heaven' as easily as or better than into a systematic theological expression."[10] In a word, God *knows* us fully, and so God simply will not let us get away (see the chapter on Ps. 23, especially on v. 6; see also Rom. 8:31–39). What amazing good news!

Questions for Reflection and Discussion

1. Some commentators conclude that certain aspects of Psalm 139 suggest that God's pervasive presence may be experienced as a threat. Do you discern a threatening aspect to Psalm 139, or is God's pervasive presence unambiguously promising and assuring?

2. Should verses 13–16 be a part of the contemporary debate over abortion? Why or why not?

3. Regardless of how you responded to question 2, what other ethical issues can be helpfully addressed from the perspective of the affirmation that human life is essentially a divine gift to be received with gratitude?

4. If you were responsible for the lectionary, would you include verses 19–22 in the reading of Psalm 139? Why or why not?

5. If possible, read the children's book by Margaret Wise Brown entitled *The Runaway Bunny*. How might this book help children (and perhaps adults as well) understand and appropriate the message of Psalm 139?

Chapter Twelve

Psalm 148

Psalm 148 is not the final psalm in the book of Psalms, but it plays a central role in bringing the Psalter to a conclusion with a crescendo of praise. A final, brief Davidic collection of psalms (Pss. 138–145) is dominated by the voice of lament and complaint, as if to recall the Davidic collections of Books I and II (Pss. 1–72), which are also dominated by lament and complaint. But Psalm 145, the final psalm in the concluding Davidic collection, contains the word "praise" in its title, suggesting that it represents a transition to Psalms 146–150, all songs of praise. But Psalms 146–150 are clearly marked as a separate concluding collection by the fact that each psalm begins and ends with the invitation *hallelujah*, "Praise the LORD!" And at the center of this concluding crescendo of praise stands Psalm 148.

Not coincidentally, it seems, the opening invitation of Psalm 146 (after the initial *hallelujah*) is "Praise the LORD, O my soul!" and the final invitation of Psalm 150 (excluding the final *hallelujah*) is "Let everything that breathes praise the LORD!" Thus, this final collection of songs of praise moves expansively from the individual self to every living creature (see the chapter on Ps. 103). Psalm 150:6, the final verse of the Psalter, demonstrates decisively and dramatically that the Psalter's invitation to praise God pushes toward universality (see also Pss. 66:1; 67:3–5; 96:1; 97:1; 99:1; 100:1; 103:19–22;

117:1), but in fact, the breath-taking invitation to "everything that breathes" is actually exceeded by Psalm 148, which invites simply *everything* to praise God, breath or no breath. So at the center of the Psalter's concluding crescendo of praise stands the extraordinarily expansive Psalm 148, inviting praise from no less than *everything*— the entire created order, animate and inanimate.

The two major sections of the psalm reinforce its ultimate inclusivity. Following the initial *hallelujah*, the opening invitation is "Praise the LORD from the heavens," and everything invited to praise God in verses 1–6 occupies the heavenly realm. The opening invitation of verse 1 is matched by verse 7, "Praise the LORD from the earth," and everything and everybody invited to praise God in verses 7–13 occupy or reside in the earthly realm. Biblically speaking, the word pair "heavens" and "earth" designates the entire created order (see Gen. 2:1, 4; Pss. 121:2; 124:8); in short, the entire creation is invited to praise God. This impressive inclusivity is reinforced even further by the nine occurrences of "all" in verses 2, 3, 9, 10, 11, and 14 (see the chapter on Ps. 103). It would be difficult to be more inclusive!

Dimensions of Meaning

Verses 1–6

Following the opening *hallelujah*, there are seven plural imperatives, inviting praise from the occupants of "the heavens" (v. 1) and from the heavens themselves ("highest heavens" in v. 4a is literally "heaven of heavens"). The number seven may be coincidental here, but it may also be another small reinforcement of the ultimate inclusivity of Psalm 148, since seven is the biblical number of wholeness or completeness. The invitation to "the heavens" and their occupants recalls Psalm 19, which begins with the affirmation that "the heavens are telling the glory of God; and the firmament proclaims his handiwork."

The occupants of "the heavens" seem to be both animate beings, namely, "angels" and "host"(v. 2; see Ps. 103:20–21), and inanimate things—"sun," "moon," "shining stars," and "waters above the heavens" (vv. 3–4). The mention of "waters above the heavens" reflects the ancient Near Eastern cosmology, which posited both waters below the earth (the source of springs and rivers) and waters above the heavenly dome or firmament (the source of rain). The list of invitees in verses 3–4 recalls the creation account in Genesis 1:1–2:4; and not surprisingly, the verb "created" (v. 5) seems to allude to Genesis 1:1–2:4, as does the affirmation that God spoke the world into being (although the verb "command" does not occur in Gen. 1:1–2:4).

Verses 5–6 form the conclusion to the first section of the psalm. Although the verb "praise" occurs again in verse 5, its form differs from the imperatives of verses 1–4, and verse 5a is repeated in verse 13a to mark the conclusion of the second section of the psalm as well. Verse 5a invites praise for God's "name" (see Pss. 8:1, 9; 23:3; 29:2; 135:1, 3, 13), suggesting God's fundamental character. Thus, Psalm 148 affirms that *who God is* is revealed by *what God does*—in this case, creating the entire cosmos. As Daniel Migliore puts it, "Creation fittingly expresses the true character of God, who is love."[1] In short, the creation itself is an act of love, affirming the good news that God loves the world, including all its creatures and all its features.

Verses 7–13

Whereas verses 1–6 invite praise "from the heavens" (v. 1), verses 7–13 invite praise "from the earth" (v. 7). The invitees are again both animate and inanimate, and as in verses 1–6, several of them recall Genesis 1:1–2:4: "sea monsters" (v. 7; see Gen. 1:21; Pss. 74:13; 89:9–10; Isa. 51:9–10), "fruit trees" (v. 9; see Gen. 1:11), "wild animals" (v. 10; see Gen. 1:24–25), "cattle" (v. 10; see Gen. 1:24–25), "creeping things" (v. 10; see Gen. 1:24), "birds" (v. 10; see Gen. 1:20), and, of course, people (vv. 11–12; see Gen. 1:26–27). Unlike verses 1–6, verses 7–13 contain only one imperative form of the verb "praise," and it is the very first word in this section. This fact, along with the much longer list of invitees in verses 7–12 (a total of twenty-three), leads Erhard Gerstenberger to conclude that "the text is crowded."[2] But perhaps this is precisely the poet's intended point. A world-encompassing crowd, consisting of both the creatures and the features God has made, is invited to praise God.

Gerstenberger detects in the list of invitees "a sort of hierarchy, from mythical powers [v. 7], superhuman forces of nature [v. 8], down to human society [vv. 11–12]," and this seems to be correct.[3] Given the numerous allusions to Genesis 1:1–2:4, it is noticeable that the list in verses 7–12 moves toward and concludes with humanity, as does the order of creation in Genesis 1. Whereas the effect in Genesis 1 is to portray the creation of humankind as the culminating act of God's creative work, such is not the case in Psalm 148. For instance, Psalm 148 does not mention "dominion" (see Gen. 1:26, 28), and even though the language of power is not absent (see "kings," "princes," and "rulers" in v. 11), the traditionally powerful folk are no more worthy or noteworthy than the ordinary people mentioned in verse 12: "Young men and women . . . old and young." As Konrad Schaefer aptly observes, "All are equal in God's sight."[4]

Indeed, this equality in God's sight seems to apply not only to the community of humankind but also to the larger, world-encompassing community consisting of all the invitees listed in verses 7–10: "sea monsters," meteorological phenomena, earth's topological features, plants, and all kinds of animals. If all these are not strictly equal to humankind in God's sight, they at least have an integrity and place of their own in the extraordinarily expansive congregation invited by Psalm 148 to praise God. As do verses 1–6, verses 7–13 clearly affirm that God claims and loves the world, the whole world, including all its features and all its creatures, human and nonhuman alike. The ecological implications are profound, and we shall consider them further below.

As we have seen, verse 13a repeats verse 5a, thus bringing the second section to a close in a way that is identical to the conclusion of the first section. God's "name" or character receives even further emphasis by virtue of a second occurrence of "name" in verse 13—God's "name be exalted." The word translated "exalted" here occurs in Isaiah 33:5 in the context of an affirmation of God's sovereignty (see Isa. 33:17–22), and "glory" also serves elsewhere as an attribute of kingship, divine (see Pss. 96:6; 145:5) and human (see Pss. 21:5; 45:3). In essence, then, verse 13 affirms God's sovereign claim over "earth and heaven," thus recalling the two major sections of the psalm. In short, God rules the universe!

Indeed, it is the affirmation of God's universal sovereignty that is the theological foundation for concluding that "all are equal in God's sight." That is, if God "alone" (v. 13) is truly sovereign, then the sovereign claim of anything or anyone other than God is relativized. In God's sight, "kings of the earth" and "princes" and "all rulers" (v. 11) are no more important than any "young men and women" or "old and young together." Thus, God's sovereign claim has a pervasive leveling effect. All people, indeed all creatures and features of creation as well, constitute a worshiping community that God claims and values. If anything like human "dominion" is asserted, as it is elsewhere (see Gen. 1:26, 28; Ps. 8:6; the Hebrew words translated "dominion" differ in these two texts), Psalm 148 insists that such dominion must be understood not as ultimate power over but rather as responsibility toward— in particular, the human responsibility to see to it that all creatures and features of God's world are preserved, so that they may take their rightful place in the universe-encompassing community of praise envisioned and invited by the psalmist.

Verse 14

Given the spectacular inclusivity of verses 1–13, it appears at first sight that verse 14 should not be the concluding verse of this psalm. Suddenly and unexpectedly, it introduces a clear note of particularity with its reference to "his people" and "his faithful" and "the people of Israel who are close to him." In view of verses 1–13, the reader may rightly wonder, "Are not all people, indeed all creatures and features of creation, close to him?" A purely historical or ideological approach to Psalm 148 might posit that Psalm 148 is a late poetic composition of the Persian or even Greek period, and that it was designed to tell the postexilic community what it wanted to believe—that is, that this embattled and oppressed minority amid the world's major empires was the special people of the universally sovereign God (see the chapter on Psalm 90 and how Books IV–V respond to the crisis of exile and its aftermath). The affirmation that God "has raised up a horn for his people" seems to lean in this interpretive direction, since the image suggests being honored or strengthened, sometimes instead of, or even at the expense of, one's enemies (see Pss. 75:10; 89:17; 92:10; 112:9). If one follows this interpretive line, then the somewhat elusive phrase "praise for all his faithful" could be interpreted as reference to Israel as a privileged people, as opposed to other peoples or nations.

In contrast to such a historical or ideological approach, a more theological approach is commended by the shape of the final form of the Old Testament, including the opening chapters of the book of Genesis, to which Psalm 148 alludes. It is significant, for instance, that Scripture begins not with Israel's story in particular but rather with the creation of the world and all humanity. The first covenant narrated in the Bible is not between God and Israel but involves God, humanity, "every living creature" (Gen. 9:9, 12, 15, 16), and "the earth" itself (Gen. 9:13). Even when the biblical story narrows its focus to Abraham, Sarah, and their descendants, the larger picture is still in view. The promise of blessing to Abraham and his descendants is accompanied by a broader promise, which at least implicitly is also a commission: "and in you all the families of the earth shall be blessed" (Gen. 12:3). In short, particularity is intended here to serve God's universal purpose, and this dynamic is an apt clue for understanding the concluding verse of Psalm 148. The clear implication of this interpretive direction is that God's particular people are called and strengthened to effect a blessing for the entire universe, not only all people but also all creatures and all features of the earth. From this perspective, Israel's "praise" is not a privileged status but rather a sacred responsibility, a divinely ordained mission to enable the whole creation to participate in praising God. As Terence Fretheim concludes, "God is enthroned not simply on the praises of Israel [see Ps. 22:3]; God is enthroned on the praises of his creatures." Thus, it follows logically that Psalm 148 "contains an implicit call to human beings to relate to the natural orders in such a way that nature's praise might show forth with greater clarity."[5] The ecological implications are of paramount importance, and we turn to them at this point.

Psalm 148 for Today

It would be anachronistic, of course, to call the poet of Psalm 148 an environmentalist, but there is no doubt that Psalm 148 lays an impressive theological foundation for what we today would call environmentalism, or ecological responsibility, or more recently, thinking and acting "green." Indeed, along with other Old Testament texts such as Genesis 1–9 and Psalms 8, 24, and 104, Psalm 148 demonstrates that from a biblical perspective, theology and ecology are inseparable. Quite simply from a biblical perspective, the world belongs to God, not to us human beings. God takes pleasure in, God loves the whole creation in all its marvelous, beautiful, intricate, and interconnected variety. And so, according to Psalm 148, God will be praised by nothing short of a cosmic congregation, consisting not only of people but also of all creatures and features of the universe. If this does not imply a strict equality among humankind, the nonhuman creatures, the plant world, and the inanimate features of creation, it should at least lead us to think in terms of what Fretheim calls a "symbiosis in praise," involving people, animals, plants, and, generally speaking, the environment.[6] It is this "symbiosis in praise" that constitutes the "implicit call to human beings to relate to the natural orders in such a way that nature's praise might show forth with greater clarity."

To be more pointed and specific, nature's praise must surely be muted when layers of smog descend upon beautiful hills and scenic valleys, not only obscuring the sun's light but also endangering the health of humans, animals, and plants. Nature's praise must surely be muted when acid rain kills the fir trees on the peaks of the Blue Ridge Mountains and the Great Smokies, and when whole mountainsides or mountaintops disappear as a result of strip mining operations. Nature's praise must surely be muted as global warming takes its increasingly more evident toll: polar bears and penguins struggle to find a liveable habitat as polar ice melts at unprecedented rates; pine beetles, no longer held in check by hard winter freezes, decimate the green expanses of forest in the Rocky Mountains of Colorado; rivers and lakes disappear and/or their levels and flows are drastically reduced; cycles of severe weather grow more frequent, intense, and destructive. Nature's praise must surely be muted as species of plants and animals disappear at alarming and unprecedented rates. To be sure, species have always become extinct, but the current rate is reliably estimated to be ten times or more higher than has been the case historically and would be the case without human interference. All of the above and more point toward the failure of us human beings to relate to our environment—that is, to God's creation—"in such a way that nature's praise might show forth with greater clarity."

The current environmental crisis is receiving a tremendous amount of attention today in the scientific community, in the media, and in the marketplace—and rightfully so! This means that Psalm 148 may be particularly timely today, since its invitation to praise also invites attention to the poet's vision of a world in which every creature and feature of creation has its own integrity and its own rightful place. At the same time, Psalm 148 may expose some of the motivation to "go green" as essentially selfish, shallow, and shortsighted, as an earlier assessment I made suggests:

> It is important to realize that much of our concern for the future of the earth is motivated by our desire to maintain our current standard of living without trashing things so terribly or depleting natural resources so severely that we cannot pass the same style of life on to our children. In other words, our primary concern is ourselves, and our major motivation is fear. While this kind of environmental consciousness may be better than none at all, our efforts to "save" the earth are surely misguided and doomed to failure as long as the focus is ourselves and our motivation is fear.[7]

Psalm 148 has the potential to ground our ecological awareness and activity in something other than ourselves. In other words, we are called to care for the earth, all its creatures, and all its features *for God's sake!* Such an awareness might help us to recognize and take more seriously something we often ignore—namely, our own creatureliness. In Hebrew, there is an unmistakable etymological connection between the words for "humanity" (*'ādām*) and "ground" (*'ădāmâ*). The etymological connection communicates the profound truth that we human beings are creatures, and that our origin, our current well-being, and a liveable human future are inextricably bound up with the past, present, and future of the earth itself. Although we seldom recognize it, our English language contains the same etymological connection and recognition by way of a Latin root: *humus*—that is, soil or dirt—and *human*.

Our past propensity to ignore the well-being of the earth, along with some of the solutions proposed for the current environmental crisis (for instance, colonizing the moon or some other location in space), suggest that we human beings often act as if we have no limits—in short, we act as if *we* are sovereign rather than acknowledging *God's* sovereignty. Such idolatry is proving to be disastrous and potentially catastrophic. What we desperately need is precisely what Psalm 148 invites—that is, the recognition of God's sovereign claim upon "earth and heaven" (v. 13). Indeed, such a recognition is the essence of praise, which is both a liturgical act and a style of life. Praise in worship involves our profession that God, "not we ourselves" (see Ps. 100:3, NRSV note), rules the world. Praise as a style of life involves the living out of what we affirm in worship—that is, living in such a way that acknowledges and preserves the value and integrity of all people, all creatures, and all features of the world God has created. In a profound sense, the solution to the current ecological crisis begins with our faithful response to the invitation of Psalm 148, "Praise the LORD!"

While a primary value of Psalm 148 for today may be to affirm the inseparability of theology and ecology, it also has important implications for the structuring of the human community. When Schaefer observes that "all are equal in God's sight," he is referring explicitly to human beings (see vv. 11–12). Although the Declaration of Independence proclaims that "all men are created equal," it is evident that very few people actually believe this, or at least act like they believe it. If we as a nation did believe in the inherent equality of every person, there would be a far greater sense of interdependence or solidarity in our country, evidenced by concern for the poor, the unemployed, and the uninsured, or perhaps just by a healthy sense of neighborliness and community. As it is, sociologists are telling us that we are plagued by a loss of what they call "social capital," by which they mean the breakdown of community and communal institutions that bring people together and keep them together.[8] Primary evidence of our loss of social capital is the excessive individualism that characterizes our culture, often accompanied by a sense of entitlement as well as things such as loneliness, isolation, and alienation (see the chapter on Ps. 1).

In their book *Better Together: Restoring the American Community*, Robert Putnam and Lewis Feldstein identify two types of social capital: "bonding social capital," which is ordinarily characteristic of relatively small, homogenous groups of people; and "bridging social capital," which involves the bringing together of diverse folk into larger communities. As they point out, bridging social capital is more difficult to obtain, because it involves difference and diversity. But in our contemporary context, bridging social capital is crucial. As Putnam and Feldstein put it, "The kind of social capital that is most essential for healthy public life in an increasingly diverse society like ours is precisely the kind that is hardest to build—that is, bridging social capital."[9]

While Psalm 148 may not make it any easier to build bridging social capital, it certainly does offer a profoundly important theological foundation for making the effort—namely, the affirmation that all are equal in God's sight. If we believe and attempt to act upon this simple affirmation, then exclusionary thinking and practice should be out of the question. Of course, from the perspective of Psalm 148, an attempt at restoring the *American* community is far too limited a goal. Rather, Psalm 148 invites an attempt at restoring the *human* community. If society in the United States is characterized by increasing diversity, it is even more so with human society on a worldwide scale, and such extraordinary diversity often becomes an occasion for hostility, divisiveness, and even war. As we have seen concerning the ecological crisis, what we desperately need is precisely what Psalm 148 invites—that is, the recognition of God's sovereign claim upon "all peoples" (v. 11). In a profound sense, the solution to the current human crisis begins with our faithful response to the invitation of Psalm 148, "Praise the LORD!"

Questions for Reflection and Discussion

1. Like other songs of praise in the Psalter, Psalm 148 proclaims God's sovereignty on a universal scale. Jesus also proclaimed the reign of God as a present reality, and he invited people to enter it (see Mark 1:14–15). How might we be more aware daily of living in the reign of God—that is, more aware of living under God's sovereign claim? And what difference will this make? In other words, what will praise look like for you when it becomes a style of life?

2. In one translation of the famous hymn "All Creatures of Our God and King," by St. Francis of Assisi, the features of creation (sun, moon, wind, waters) are addressed as "brother" and "sister." How does this help to capture the message and spirit of Psalm 148? If you have access to them in your hymnal, see also "Let All Things Now Living" by Katherine K. Davis and "Earth and All Stars" by Herbert F. Brokering and discuss them in relation to Psalm 148.

3. In his book *The Diversity of Life* Edward O. Wilson points out that if all the insects and bugs in the world were to disappear suddenly, human life would be able to exist on earth for only a matter of months. Does this help you to appreciate the biblical account of the first covenant, which included "every living creature" (Gen. 9:9, 12, 15, 16)? Might it be helpful in some sense also to think about bugs and insects as our brothers and sisters?

4. In what kinds of ecological activities are you involved? What motivates your ecological thinking and acting? Does the kind of theological foundation provided by Psalm 148 help? Why or why not?

5. In some contemporary liturgical circles, "praise music" has a bad reputation because it often seems musically monotonous and focused theologically on the faith experiences of individual persons. What kind of "praise music" does Psalm 148 offer and/or inspire?

Notes

1. Psalm 1

1. Jon Levenson, "The Sources of Torah: Psalm 119 and the Modes of Revelation in Second Temple Judaism," in *Ancient Israelite Religion*, ed. P. D. Miller, P. D. Hanson, S. D. McBride (Philadelphia: Fortress Press, 1987), 570.
2. Klaus Seybold, *Introducing the Psalms*, trans. R. G. Dunphy (Edinburgh: T. & T. Clark, 1990), 27.
3. James L. Mays, *Preaching and Teaching the Psalms*, ed. P. D. Miller and G. M. Tucker, Interpretation (Louisville, KY: Westminster John Knox Press, 2006), 69–70.
4. Jerome Creach, *The Destiny of the Righteous in the Psalms* (St. Louis: Chalice Press, 2008), 3.
5. Brevard Childs, *Old Testament Theology in a Canonical Context* (Philadelphia: Fortress Press, 1985), 56.
6. Creach, *The Destiny of the Righteous*, 143.
7. Walker Percy, *Lost in the Cosmos: The Last Self-Help Book* (New York: Washington Square Press, 1983), 12
8. *Time*, December 26, 2006/January 1, 2007, 40–41.
9. James Poniewozik, "The Age of iPod Politics: The Niching of America Makes for Happy Consumers and Angry Voters," *Time*, September 27, 2004, 84.
10. "'Me Decade' Celebrates 35th Year," *Onion*, March 9, 2005, http://www.theonion.com/content/node/33052.
11. Mary Pipher, *The Shelter of Each Other: Rebuilding Our Families* (New York: Ballantine Books, 1996), 26.
12. James C. Edwards, *The Plain Sense of Things: The Fate of Religion in an Age of Normal Nihilism* (University Park: Pennsylvania State University Press, 1997), 49.
13. Ibid., 53; see 52–54.

14. Pipher, *Shelter of Each Other*, 113.
15. Steve Fazzari and Barry Cynamon, editorial, *St. Louis Post-Dispatch*, October 3, 2007, B9.

2. Psalm 8

1. See James Limburg, *Psalms*, Westminster Bible Companion (Louisville, KY: Westminster John Knox Press, 2000), 24.
2. See Suzanne Haïk Vantoura, *The Music of the Bible Revealed*, trans. Dennis Weber, ed. John Wheeler (Berkeley, CA: Bibal Press, 1991). An Internet search will put one in touch with recordings of Vantoura's work, including postings on YouTube.
3. John Goldingay, *Psalms*, vol. 1, *Psalms 1–41*, Baker Commentary on the Old Testament Wisdom and Psalms (Grand Rapids: Baker Academic, 2006), 156.
4. See Konrad Schaefer, *Psalms*, Berit Olam: Studies in Hebrew Narrative and Poetry (Collegeville, MN: Liturgical Press, 2001), 24.
5. See Robert Alter, *The Art of Biblical Poetry* (New York: Basic Books, 1985), 119.
6. Walter Brueggemann, *The Message of the Psalms* (Minneapolis: Augsburg, 1984), 37–38.
7. Limburg, *Psalms*, 26. See also James Limburg, "Who Cares for the Earth? Psalm 8 and the Environment," *Word and World Supplement Series* 1 (1992): 43–52.
8. Douglas John Hall, *God and Human Suffering: An Exercise in the Theology of the Cross* (Minneapolis: Augsburg, 1986), 71.
9. Ibid., 70.
10. For an explanation of this translation, see J. Gerald Janzen, *Job*, Interpretation: A Bible Commentary for Teaching and Preaching (Atlanta: John Knox Press, 1985), 254–59.
11. James L. Mays, *Preaching and Teaching the Psalms*, ed. P. D. Miller and G. M. Tucker, Interpretation (Louisville, KY: Westminster John Knox Press, 2006), 67.
12. Ibid., 105.

3. Psalm 13

1. James L. Mays, "Psalm 13," *Interpretation* 34 (1980): 279.
2. Quoted in Eugene Peterson, *Answering God: The Psalms as Tools for Prayer* (San Francisco: Harper & Row, 1989), 36.
3. Robert Alter, *The Art of Biblical Poetry* (New York: Basic Books, 1985), 65.
4. Erhard Gerstenberger, *Psalms, Part 1, with an Introduction to Cultic Poetry*, Forms of the Old Testament Literature 14 (Grand Rapids: Wm. B. Eerdmans, 1988), 84.
5. James L. Mays, *The Lord Reigns: A Theological Handbook to the Psalms* (Louisville, KY: Westminster John Knox Press, 1994), 37.
6. Mays, "Psalm 13," 281–82.

7. Mary Pipher, *The Shelter of Each Other: Rebuilding Our Families* (New York: G. P. Putnam's Sons, 1996), 143.
8. Ibid., 119.
9. James L. Mays, *Preaching and Teaching the Psalms*, ed. P. D. Miller and G. M. Tucker (Louisville, KY: Westminster John Knox Press, 2006), 184.
10. Walter Brueggemann, "The Costly Loss of Lament," *Journal for the Study of the Old Testament* 36 (1986): 57–71.
11. John Calvin, *Commentary on the Book of Psalms*, vol. 1 (Edinburgh: Calvin Translation Society, 1845; repr., Baker Book House), xxxix.
12. Stephanie Knopf, "Psalms as a Resource for Those Grieving the Loss of a Loved One," master's thesis, Eden Theological Seminary, May 2007.

4. Psalm 23

1. William L. Holladay, *The Psalms through Three Thousand Years: Prayerbook of a Cloud of Witnesses* (Minneapolis: Fortress Press, 1993), 359.
2. Walter Brueggemann, *The Message of the Psalms* (Minneapolis: Augsburg, 1984), 154.
3. Philip Jenkins, "Liberating Word: The Power of the Bible in the Global South," *Christian Century*, July 11, 2006, 26.
4. Gerald H. Wilson, *Psalms*, vol. 1, NIV Application Commentary (Grand Rapids: Zondervan, 2002), 432.
5. Ibid., 433.
6. Isaac Watts, 1719, altered 1972, in *Hymns, Songs, and Spiritual Songs* (Louisville, KY: Westminster John Knox Press, 1990), no. 172.
7. Henri Nouwen, *Gracias! A Latin American Journal* (Maryknoll, NY: Orbis Books, 1993), 187.
8. Thomas Merton, *The Springs of Contemplation: A Retreat at the Abbey of Gethsemani* (Notre Dame, IN: Ave Maria Press, 1997), 110.
9. Quoted in Phyllis Tickle, *Greed: The Seven Deadly Sins* (New York: Oxford University Press, 2004), 18.
10. Nouwen, *Gracias!*, 188.
11. This is essentially the argument of Elsa Tamez in *The Amnesty of Grace: Justification by Faith from a Latin American Perspective*, trans. Sharon Ringe (Nashville: Abingdon Press, 1993), 134–40.
12. Konrad Schaefer, *Psalms*, Berit Olam: Studies in Hebrew Narrative and Poetry (Collegeville, MN: Liturgical Press, 2001), 59.
13. M. Douglas Meeks, *God the Economist: The Doctrine of God and Political Economy* (Minneapolis: Fortress Press, 1989), 180.
14. Walter Brueggemann, "What Would Jesus Buy?" *Sojourners*, November 2007, 8.
15. Ibid., 15.
16. Wilson, *Psalms*, 445.

5. Psalm 32

1. James Limburg, *Psalms*, Westminster Bible Companion (Louisville, KY: Westminster John Knox Press, 2000), 105.

2. Rowland E. Prothero, *The Psalms in Human Life* (New York: E. P. Dutton, 1903), 29.

3. Konrad Schaefer, *Psalms*, Berit Olam: Studies in Hebrew Narrative and Poetry (Collegeville, MN: Liturgical Press, 2001), 79.

4. Robert Jenson, "Psalm 32," *Interpretation* 33 (1979): 175.

5. Erhard Gerstenberger, *Psalms, Part 1, with an Introduction to Cultic Poetry*, Forms of the Old Testament Literature 14 (Grand Rapids: Wm. B. Eerdmans, 1988), 143.

6. John Goldingay, *Psalms*, vol. 1, *Psalms 1–41*, Baker Commentary on the Old Testament Wisdom and Psalms (Grand Rapids: Baker Academic, 2006), 453.

7. Ibid., 455.

8. James L. Mays, *Psalms*, Interpretation: A Bible Commentary for Teaching and Preaching (Louisville, KY: John Knox Press, 1994), 147.

9. Limburg, *Psalms*, 104–5.

10. Gerstenberger, *Psalms, Part 1*, 141.

11. Diane Santelli, untitled sermon on Psalm 32, preached at Hope United Church of Christ, St. Louis, Missouri, March 18, 2007.

12. Karl Menninger, *Whatever Became of Sin?* (New York: Hawthorn, 1973), 178.

13. Ibid., 192.

14. Gerald H. Wilson, *Psalms*, vol. 1, NIV Application Commentary (Grand Rapids: Zondervan, 2002), 551.

15. Ibid.

16. Ibid., 552.

17. Ibid.

18. Fredrick Buechner, *Telling Secrets: A Memoir* (San Francisco: HarperSanFrancisco, 1991), 93.

19. Mark E. Biddle, *Missing the Mark: Sin and Its Consequences in Biblical Theology* (Nashville: Abingdon Press, 2005), 138.

6. Psalm 51

1. James Limburg, *Psalms*, Westminster Bible Companion (Louisville, KY: Westminster John Knox Press, 2000), 172.

2. See Michael Goulder, *The Prayers of David (Psalms 51–72): Studies in the Psalter II*, Journal for the Study of the Old Testament Supplement Series 102 (Sheffield: JSOT Press, 1990), 24–30, 51–69.

3. Konrad Schaefer, *Psalms*, Berit Olam: Studies in Hebrew Narrative and Poetry (Collegeville, MN: Liturgical Press, 2001), 131.

4. Ibid.

5. Ibid., 129.

6. Douglas John Hall, *God and Human Suffering: An Exercise in the Theology of the Cross* (Minneapolis: Augsburg, 1986), 77–78.

7. "A Call to Lament and Repent: Guide Our Feet to the Path of Peace," http://www.sojo.net/action/alerts/080307_paths_of_peace.html.

8. Nancy Gibbs, "The New Road to Hell," *Time*, March 24, 2008, 78.

9. Gerald H. Wilson, *Psalms*, vol. 1, NIV Application Commentary (Grand Rapids: Zondervan, 2002), 783.

10. William C. Placher, "Christ Takes Our Place: Rethinking Atonement," *Interpretation* 53, no. 1 (January 1999): 15.

11. Walter Brueggemann, *Like Fire in the Bones: Listening for the Prophetic Word in Jeremiah*, ed. P. D. Miller (Minneapolis: Fortress Press, 2006), 193.

12. Shirley C. Guthrie, *Always Being Reformed: Faith for a Fragmented World* (Louisville, KY: Westminster John Knox Press, 1996), 83.

7. Psalm 63

1. Konrad Schaefer, *Psalms*, Berit Olam: Studies in Hebrew Narrative and Poetry (Collegeville, MN: Liturgical Press, 2001), 152.

2. Rowland E. Prothero, *The Psalms in Human Life and Experience* (New York: E. P. Dutton, 1903), 77, 141.

3. James L. Mays, *Psalms*, Interpretation: A Bible Commentary for Teaching and Preaching (Louisville, KY: John Knox Press, 1994), 218.

4. See the *Book of Common Worship* (Louisville, KY: Westminster John Knox Press, 1993), 68.

5. Claus Westermann, *Praise and Lament in the Psalms*, trans. K. R. Crim and R. N. Soulen (Atlanta: John Knox Press, 1981), 160–61.

6. See *Guatemala: Never Again! Recovery of Historical Memory Project—The Official Report of the Human Rights Office, Archdiocese of Guatemala* (Maryknoll, NY: Orbis Books, 1999). José Antonio Puac is listed on p. ii as one of the "Diocesan Coordinators."

7. Julia Esquivel, *Threatened with Resurrection: Prayers and Poems from an Exiled Guatemalan*, 2nd ed. (Elgin, IL: Brethren Press, 1994), 58–65.

8. Mays, *Psalms*, 218.

9. Gerald H. Wilson, *Psalms*, vol. 1, NIV Application Commentary (Grand Rapids: Zondervan, 2002), 895.

10. Harlan Spector, "Suicide Rising among Middle-Aged in NE Ohio," *Cleveland [OH] Plain Dealer*, March 27, 2008, A8.

11. For a fuller discussion of what it means to be "evangelically poor," see Leonardo Boff and Clovis Boff, *Introducing Liberation Theology*, trans. Paul Burns (Maryknoll, NY: Orbis Books, 1987), 48–49.

8. Psalm 73

1. John Goldingay, *Psalms*, vol. 2, *Psalms 42–89*, Baker Commentary on the Old Testament Wisdom and Psalms (Grand Rapids: Baker Academic, 2007), 419.

2. F.-L. Hossfeld and Erich Zenger, *Psalms 2*, Hermeneia (Minneapolis: Fortress Press, 2005), 238.

3. Ibid., 237.

4. Harold Kushner, *When Bad Things Happen to Good People* (New York: Avon, 1981).

5. Erhard Gerstenberger, *Psalms, Part 2, and Lamentations*, Forms of the Old Testament Literature 15 (Grand Rapids: Wm. B. Eerdmans, 2001), 74.

6. Konrad Schaefer, *Psalms*, Berit Olam: Studies in Hebrew Narrative and Poetry (Collegeville, MN: Liturgical Press, 2001), 177.
7. Walter Brueggemann, "Bounded by Obedience and Praise: The Psalms as Canon," *Journal for the Study of the Old Testament* 50 (1991): 81.
8. Goldingay, *Psalms*, vol. 2, 404.
9. James Limburg, *Psalms*, Westminster Bible Companion (Louisville, KY: Westminster John Knox Press, 2000), 248.
10. Schaefer, *Psalms*, 181.
11. Brueggemann, "Bounded by Obedience and Praise," 86.
12. William C. Placher, *Narratives of a Vulnerable God: Christ, Theology, and Scripture* (Louisville, KY: Westminster John Knox Press, 1994), 178.

9. Psalm 90

1. James L. Mays, *Psalms*, Interpretation: A Bible Commentary for Teaching and Preaching (Louisville, KY: John Knox Press, 1994), 292.
2. F.-L. Hossfeld and Erich Zenger, *Psalms 2*, Hermeneia (Minneapolis: Fortress Press, 2005), 422, 419.
3. James Limburg, *Psalms*, Westminster Bible Companion (Louisville, KY: Westminster John Knox Press, 2000), 309–10.
4. Hossfeld and Zenger, *Psalms 2*, 423.
5. See *The New Century Hymnal* (Cleveland: Pilgrim Press, 1995), no. 607.
6. John Goldingay, *Psalms*, vol. 1, *Psalms 1–41*, Baker Commentary on the Old Testament Wisdom and Psalms (Grand Rapids: Baker Academic, 2006), 565.
7. Reinhold Niebuhr, *The Irony of American History* (New York: Charles Scribner's Sons, 1952), 63.
8. Quoted in James B. Dunning, *Echoing God's Word: Formation for Catechists and Homilitists in a Catechumenal Church* (Arlington, VA: North American Forum on the Catechumenate, 1992), 380.

10. Psalm 103

1. James Limburg, *Psalms*, Westminster Bible Companion (Louisville, KY: Westminster John Knox Press, 2000), 350.
2. Konrad Schaefer, *Psalms*, Berit Olam: Studies in Hebrew Narrative and Poetry (Collegeville, MN: Liturgical Press, 2001), 256.
3. James L. Mays, *Psalms*, Interpretation: A Bible Commentary for Teaching and Preaching (Louisville, KY: John Knox Press, 1994), 336.
4. See Phyllis Trible, *God and the Rhetoric of Sexuality*, Overtures to Biblical Theology (Philadelphia: Fortress Press, 1978), 38–53.
5. Artur Weiser, *The Psalms*, trans. H. Hartwell, Old Testament Library (Philadelphia: Westminster Press, 1962), 663.
6. See Barclay M. Newman, Charles S. Houser, Erroll F. Rhodes, and David G. Burke, *Creating and Crafting the Contemporary English Version* (New York: American Bible Society, 1996), 26–29.
7. Claus Westermann, *Elements of Old Testament Theology*, trans. D. W. Stott (Atlanta: John Knox Press, 1982), 139.
8. Erhard Gerstenberger, *Psalms, Part 2, and Lamentations*, Forms of the

Old Testament Literature 15 (Grand Rapids: Wm. B. Eerdmans, 2001), 200.

9. Schaefer, *Psalms*, 256.

11. Psalm 139

1. Erhard Gerstenberger, *Psalms, Part 2, and Lamentations*, Forms of the Old Testament Literature 15 (Grand Rapids: Wm. B. Eerdmans, 2001), 404.
2. Konrad Schaefer, *Psalms*, Berit Olam: Studies in Hebrew Narrative and Poetry (Collegeville, MN: Liturgical Press, 2001), 328.
3. Gerstenberger, *Psalms, Part 2*, 407.
4. Ibid., 402.
5. John Calvin, *Commentary on the Book of Psalms*, vol. 1 (Edinburgh: Calvin Translation Society, 1845; repr. Baker Book House), 369.
6. For a more extensive treatment of the issue, see J. Clinton McCann Jr., "Toward a Nonretaliatory Lifestyle: The Psalms, the Cross, and the Gospel," in *Character Ethics and the New Testament: Moral Dimensions of Scripture*, ed. Robert L. Brawley (Louisville, KY: Westminster John Knox Press, 2007), 159–67. See also Erich Zenger, *A God of Vengeance? Understanding the Psalms of Enmity*, trans. Linda Maloney (Louisville, KY: Westminster John Knox Press, 1995).
7. C. S. Lewis, *Reflections on the Psalms* (New York: Harcourt, Brace & Co., 1958), 24.
8. James Limburg, *Psalms*, Westminster Bible Companion (Louisville, KY: Westminster John Knox Press, 2000), 471.
9. Walter Brueggemann, *Praying the Psalms* (Winona, MN: St. Mary's Press, 1982), 68.
10. Patrick D. Miller, *Interpreting the Psalms* (Philadelphia: Fortress Press, 1986), 144.

12. Psalm 148

1. Daniel L. Migliore, *Faith Seeking Understanding: An Introduction to Christian Theology* (Grand Rapids: Wm. B. Eerdmans, 1991), 84.
2. Erhard Gerstenberger, *Psalms, Part 2, and Lamentations*, Forms of the Old Testament Literature 15 (Grand Rapids: Wm. B. Eerdmans, 2001), 449.
3. Ibid.
4. Konrad Schaefer, *Psalms*, Berit Olam: Studies in Hebrew Narrative and Poetry (Collegeville, MN: Liturgical Press, 2001), 343.
5. Terence E. Fretheim, "Nature's Praise of God in the Psalms," *Ex Auditu* 3 (1987): 29.
6. Ibid., 28.
7. J. Clinton McCann Jr., "The Book of Psalms: Introduction, Commentary, and Reflections," in *The New Interpreter's Bible*, vol. 4 (Nashville: Abingdon Press, 1996), 1100.
8. See, for instance, Robert D. Putnam, *Bowling Alone: The Collapse and Revival of American Community* (New York: Simon & Schuster, 2000), 15–28.
9. Robert D. Putnam and Lewis M. Feldstein, *Better Together: Restoring the American Community* (New York: Simon & Schuster, 2003), 3.